Cellar & Silver
ENTERTAINING AT HOME

with
Rose Murray & Tony Aspler

Happy Entertaining

Rose Murray

McGraw-Hill Ryerson
Toronto   Montreal

First published in 1993 by
McGraw-Hill Ryerson Limited
300 Water Street
Whitby, Ontario, Canada
LIN 9B6

Canadian Cataloguing in Publication Data

Murray, Rose, 1941-
   Cellar and silver : entertaining at home

ISBN 0-07-551562-8

I. Menus. 2. Cookery. 3. Entertaining.
I. Aspler, Tony, 1939-   . II. Title.

TX731.M87 1993   642'.4   C93-094052-0

Produced by B & E Publications Inc.
Suite 265
7025 Tomken Road
Mississauga, Ontario
L5S IR6

Design by B & E Publications Inc.
Front and back cover photos by Tom Bakowsky
Printed and bound in Canada

For Kent who helps make entertaining
easy and enjoyable.

R.M.

For my daughter Annabel.

T.A.

Contents

The Food

*A*s I was growing up, our big farmhouse seemed always full of people. There were relatives and friends who happily came from far and near to enjoy my mother's good food, my father's great sense of humor and our home's hospitable aura. I grew up in a family for which entertaining was a natural way of life.

In my own home, in which I love to cook for other people, I have a husband who enjoys playing host and two gregarious children so that entertaining continues to be important.

Having friends in is not always a formal occasion at our house. Sometimes, I call our close friend Edna a few hours before Sunday's roast chicken dinner because I remember she loves it. Or, I'm testing a menu for a magazine and use a few good friends as guinea pigs. And when there is a special occasion, I invite only people I really like and prepare food that I like to cook and eat. This, I believe, is the cardinal rule—please *yourself* when entertaining—and everything else falls into place.

Pleasing yourself means not getting stressed out by letting your ambitions exceed your capabilities, time or economic limits. It also involves enjoying the advance preparations and, when the event comes around, having all the work done ahead so that you are not stuck in the kitchen missing out on the fun. When you do have last-minute things to do and someone offers to help, accept the help; it's much easier, and certain guests feel more comfortable helping.

As time goes on, I find the menus I use get easier and simpler, although they may sound or look more time-consuming. Since I don't like fussing too much, the recipes are very accessible and primarily make-ahead. I love parties and I don't want to miss any of my own.

And, of course, wine makes any party sparkle. Wine expert Tony Aspler makes that part of entertaining easy, too, by choosing each wine for you, while his charming comments generally help to take the mystery out of the marriage of wine and food.

It's with great pleasure that I pass along some of my favorite menus and recipes to guide you through a whole year of enjoyable entertaining so that you don't miss any of your parties.

Rose Murray

Planning & Preparation

Practical organization:

Make a list of *everything* you have to do. If you're running out of time as the party gets closer, eliminate items and you'll feel much better.

My menus are carefully thought out so that each item goes with the others, but if you don't feel like making the pizza dough for Sage Leaf Focaccia, feel free to slip out to the local pizza shop to buy some. Don't worry about making Cheddar Cornbread if time has evaporated; buy some good crusty loaves of white bread. The homemade Cinnamon Ice Cream is absolutely delicious, but if ice-cream making is not one of your regular activities, you may want to buy a good commercial flavor. Be flexible and realistic in doing what you can.

Try to set aside at least 30 minutes just for yourself before everyone arrives.

Seating plans:

If you're going to have a sit-down dinner party, set the table and get out all the serving pieces the day before. If there are more than four or six diners, I usually include place cards. They give you a chance to ponder over who sits where.

Split up couples. Often, I have more women than men at the table so I try to sprinkle the men around. As well, I am careful not to put all the dynamic people together, but intersperse them with quieter guests.

Quantity of food:

I like to have more than enough food because I often have anxiety dreams about running out of food and because I love eating leftovers the next day. However, I often find my food-loving friends are such hearty eaters that there's nothing left. That pleases me because it shows they liked what I cooked for them.

The servings I have suggested for menus and recipes are what I have found appropriate for our guests. You know your own guests and their appetites.

The Wine

The fun of entertaining is that you make that little extra effort. You and your spouse may be content with a dinner of soufflé and salad at the kitchen table, but when you invite guests into your home you tend to 'Put on the Ritz.' You want to please. The best china, the best silver, the best ingredients and, of course, the best wines. After all, the act of offering food is a gesture of love most of the time (unless you've invited your boss for dinner and the motive is to impress).

Rose Murray has created a tantalizing range of menus for a wide variety of occasions, setting specific dishes against each other to achieve balance and a harmony of taste sensations. My delectable task has been to analyze the dishes in terms of their flavor components and suggest appropriate wines to accompany the foods. Just as one dish should complement or contrast with those that follow, so the wines to be served through the meal should set off the food and build to a crescendo.

In making my selections, I have scaled the wine budget to the occasion. For instance, at Christmas and other times of celebration we tend to spend a little more on wines than we would for a party on the patio or a summer picnic. For the most part, the wines are restricted to the $10 to $25 price range, although some may be as low as $7 to $8.

The fundamental principle in choosing wine to match food is *marry quality with quality.* Just as you would be ill-advised to pull the cork of a Château Margaux 1982 for baked beans and weiners, so you should not open a screwtop litre of Bulgarian white wine with a lobster Thermidor. If you did that in a fine restaurant, the chef might take offense and emerge from the kitchen with a cleaver.

Many of us were brought up on the homily, 'Red wine with meat, white wine with fish.' A variant of this is the old saw, 'Red wine with red meat, white wine with white meat.' These so-called gustatory laws are not only very limiting, but they are also not true in enough instances to give them relevance. If you drink rosé or sparkling wine with your meal, does it mean that an enraged Bacchus will suddenly appear at your table brandishing a vine stalk? And must you foreswear wine with steak if reds give you a headache? Not at all. These old saws are merely broad rules of thumb for the conventional and the non-adventurous.

In offering wine selections for each recipe, I don't want to give the impression that there is only one suitable wine for every dish. There are, in most cases, several wine styles that would work well. In suggesting an accompanying wine, I have first offered a style that could encompass many products which are available in your local store. For instance, when I write that a particular shellfish dish calls for a 'light, bone-dry white with crisp acidity,' this definition could fit Italian Frascati, Alsatian Sylvaner, Austrian Grüner Veltliner, Loire Muscadet, Mosel Riesling, Swiss Fendant, French Chablis, French Savoie, Ontario Seyval Blanc and English Müller-Thurgau, to name but ten regional wines. If I only mention two examples to go with a given dish, this does not mean that these are the only wines fit to accompany your culinary efforts. On page 11, you will find a list that will give you substitute wines of similar style.

The examples cited after each recipe are either from a specified village and region (i.e., Sancerre [Loire]) or a particular grape variety from a designated growing area (i.e., Californian Sauvignon Blanc). Sometimes an individual producer's wines are named where this is significant and the wine in question is widely available. In addition to the imported international wines, I have also offered a Canadian option. In some cases, I have recommended aperitifs or digestifs when the occasion warrants.

I have also tried to select a single wine (where possible) that can be consumed with pleasure throughout the meal for those who would rather stick to a single bottle. For those who, for medical or organoleptic reasons, would rather stay away from red wine, I have offered a white wine suggestion where applicable.

Remember that food alters the taste of wine and vice versa. If, for instance, you try a glass of Muscadet, you may find that it is too dry or sharp for your taste. But sip the same wine with grilled sardines and you will find that its acidity cuts through the oiliness of the fish and cleanses the palate. Taken with the fish, the wine does not taste as sharp.

WINE SUBSTITUTES

Sometimes the wines suggested in this book might not be readily available to you. Or you may have something in your cellar that you would like to try with one of Rose's recipes. As I've already mentioned there is no one single perfect wine to match a dish; there are always alternatives. The main principles in marrying food and wine are weight and style. A heavy dish demands a full-bodied, gutsy wine; a delicate dish needs a light, elegant wine.

I have divided the wines of the world into styles, using a well-known, readily available wine as the model, and I have offered a catalogue of alternatives in the same style if not flavor.

WHITE:

Very dry, medium-bodied
Chablis (Chardonnay):
    Muscadet (Loire)
    Aligoté (Burgundy)
    Cortese di Gavi (Italy)
    Northern Italian Chardonnay
    Torgiano (Italy)
    Verdicchio (Italy)
    Grüner Veltliner (Austria)
    White Rioja (Spain)
    White Penedes (Spain)
    Weissburgunder (Germany)
    Fendant (Switzerland)
    N.Y./Ontario whites

Dry, medium-bodied
Mâcon-Villages (Chardonnay):
    Pinot Blanc (Alsace)
    Sancerre (Loire)
    Vouvray (dry) (Loire)
    Pinot Grigio (Italy)
    Central European Chardonnay
    Oregon Chardonnay
    Washington Chardonnay
    Côtes du Rhône white
    Bordeaux white
    Soave (Italy)
    Corvo (Sicily)
    Sauvignon Blanc (Chile)
    Apelia (Greece)

Dry, full-bodied
Puligny-Montrachet (Chardonnay):
    Californian Chardonnay
    Californian Sauvignon Blanc
    (Fumé Blanc)
    Australian Chardonnay
    New Zealand Chardonnay
    New Zealand Sauvignon Blanc
    Tokay-Pinot Gris (Alsace)
    Pouilly-Fumé (Loire)
    Condrieu (Rhône)

Medium-dry, medium-bodied
Liebfraumilch (Müller-Thurgau/Sylvaner/
    Riesling):
    Riesling (Germany/Austria)
    Sylvaner (Alsace)
    Muscat (Alsace)
    Müller-Thurgau (Germany)
    Scheurebe (Germany)
    Traminer (N. Italy/Yugoslavia)
    Riesling (Australia)
    Riesling (California)
    Chenin Blanc (Australia)
    Malvasia (Italy)
    Gewürztraminer (Washington)
    French Colombard (California)
    B.C. Riesling/Kerner

RED:

Dry, light-bodied

Beaujolais (Gamay):
> Valpolicella (Italy)
> Bardolino (Italy)
> Grignolino (Italy)
> Dolcetto
> Chinon or Bourgueil (Loire)
> Pinot Noir (Alsace)
> Clairette (Languedoc)
> German reds
> Swiss reds
> Savoie reds
> Jura reds
> Ontario Gamay Beaujolais
> B.C. reds

Dry, medium-bodied

Red Bordeaux (Cabernet Sauvignon/
> Cabernet Franc/Merlot):
> Bergerac
> Californian Cabernet Sauvignon
> California Meritage blends
> Australian Cabernet Sauvignon
> New Zealand Cabernet Sauvignon
> South African Cabernet Sauvignon
> N.Y./Ontario Cabernet Sauvignon
> Chilean Cabernet Sauvignon
> Argentinian Cabernet Sauvignon
> Spanish Cabernet Sauvignon
> Camarate, Periquita (Portugal)
> Italian Merlot

Dry, medium-bodied

Red Burgundy (Pinot Noir):
> Oregon Pinot Noir
> Californian Pinot Noir
> German Spätburgunder
> Austrian Blauburgunder
> Italian Pinot Nero
> Hungarian Nagyburgundi
> Chilean Pinot Noir
> New Zealand Pinot Noir
> South African Pinotage
> Barbera (Italy/California)
> Ontario Pinot Noir or Merlot

Dry, full-bodied

Red Rhône (Syrah, Grenache):
> Zinfandel (California)
> Petite Syrah (California)
> Primitivo (Italy)
> Barolo/Barbaresco (Italy)
> Chianti (Italy)
> Amarone (Italy)
> Castel del Monte (Italy)
> Brunello di Montalcino (Italy)
> Vino Nobile di Montepulciano (Italy)
> Sicilian reds
> Australian Shiraz/Hermitage
> South African Roodeberg
> Bull's Blood (Hungary)

The Menus

New Year's Day Dinner For Twelve

Smoked Trout Mousse on Belgian Endive Spears

Potted Goat Cheese

Roast Beef with Pan Gravy

Horseradish Sauce

Celery Mashed Potatoes

Brussels Sprouts Sautéed with Bacon

Honey-Glazed Carrots and Parsnips

Green Salad with Walnut Dressing

Cranberry Cake with White Chocolate Glaze

$\mathcal{B}$ecause we always have a house full of overnight guests during the New Year's period and celebrate New Year's Eve well into the early morning hours, I make New Year's Day dinner as simple as possible.

In my opinion, nothing is easier than sticking a big roast of beef in the oven. The other menu items are quick to prepare as well, and most can be made a day or more in advance.

PARTY PRIMER

1. *Up to three days ahead, make Potted Goat Cheese.*
2. *Up to two days ahead, make dressing for salad; wash and dry greens and toast walnuts.*
3. *One day ahead, make Smoked Trout Mousse, Celery Mashed Potatoes and Honey-Glazed Carrots and Parsnips. Make and glaze Cranberry Cake.*
4. *Early in the day, parboil Brussels sprouts; dice and refrigerate bacon.*
5. *About three hours before serving, prepare roast. Make Horseradish Sauce.*
6. *Pipe mousse into endive spears; garnish plate.*
7. *Reheat potatoes and carrot-parsnip dish. Cook bacon and finish Brussels sprouts. Make gravy.*
8. *Just before serving, toss salad with dressing.*

Smoked Trout Mousse on Belgian Endive Spears

3/4 lb	boned skinned smoked trout	375 g
1/4 cup	fresh lemon juice	50 mL
3 tbsp	each mayonnaise and whipping cream	50 mL
Pinch	each salt, pepper and cayenne	Pinch
2 or 3	heads Belgian endive, leaves separated	2 or 3
	Sprigs of fresh dill	
	Lemon wedges or slices	

Cut fish into small pieces and purée in food processor or blender. Add lemon juice, mayonnaise, whipping cream, salt, pepper and cayenne; process for 30 seconds or until smooth but not watery.

Transfer to bowl; cover and refrigerate for up to 1 day. Remove from refrigerator 30 minutes before serving.

Pipe into endive leaves and decorate each with sprig of fresh dill. Garnish plate with lemon wedges. Makes 10 to 12 servings.

Smooth, light and slightly smoky, this easy mousse perfectly complements Belgian endive leaves which have an edge of bitterness. Or, spread the mousse onto melba toast, French bread or plain crackers. Two trout, a bit over a pound (500 g) in total, should give you the right amount. If you wish, use the same amount of any other smoked fish.

THE WINE

If ever there was one wine that would do justice to fish, cheese and vegetables, it's Sauvignon Blanc from the Loire.

International option: Sancerre or Pouilly-Fumé from the Loire or Muscadet (Loire) or California Fumé Blanc.

Canadian option: Ontario Aligoté or B.C. Pinot Gris.

Potted Goat Cheese

10	cloves garlic, unpeeled	10
8 oz	soft fresh mild goat cheese	250 g
4 oz	cream cheese, softened	125 g
1 tbsp	olive oil	15 mL
2 tbsp	chopped fresh parsley	25 mL
1 tbsp	minced fresh basil (or 1 tsp/5 mL dried)	15 mL
1-1/2 tsp	each minced fresh rosemary and thyme (or 1/2 tsp/2 mL crushed dried)	7 mL
1/4 tsp	each cayenne and black pepper	1 mL

Cook garlic in simmering water until soft, about 20 minutes. Drain,

Serve in the middle of a platter surrounded with toasted baguette slices or crackers and raw vegetables like broccoli and cauliflower florets, cherry tomatoes and snow peas.

cool and peel. Transfer to food processor and chop. Add goat cheese, cream cheese and oil; blend until smooth but not liquefied.

Transfer to medium bowl; stir in parsley, basil, rosemary, thyme, cayenne and black pepper. Pack into serving crock or bowl. Cover and refrigerate at least overnight or for up to 3 days. Serve at room temperature. Makes 1-1/4 cups (300 mL).

ROAST BEEF WITH PAN GRAVY

1	standing rib roast of beef (7 to 8 lb/3.15 to 3.6 kg) Salt and pepper	1
3 tbsp	all-purpose flour	50 mL
2-1/2 cups	liquid	625 mL

A standing rib roast is truly the 'king of roasts' and forms the basis for one of the easiest dinners ever. For the gravy, use a combination of liquid from cooking vegetables, beef broth and dry red wine or just beef broth.

Place beef, rib side down, in large shallow roasting pan; sprinkle with salt and pepper. Roast, uncovered, in 450°F (230°C) oven for 20 minutes. Reduce temperature to 325°F (160°C) and roast for about 15 minutes a pound (500 g) or until meat thermometer reaches 140°F (60°C) for rare.

Transfer beef to cutting board and let stand under tent of foil for 20 minutes before carving.

Skim fat from pan drippings; stir in flour and cook over medium heat for 1 minute, stirring constantly. Gradually stir in liquid and any juice from meat; bring to boil, stirring up any brown bits. Reduce heat and simmer for 5 minutes or until thickened. Season to taste with salt and pepper. Pass in heated sauceboat with roast. Makes 12 servings.

THE WINE

The wine you choose with simple roasted beef depends on whether you like the meat rare or medium-to-well-done. If rare, choose a young red with some tannin. If on the well-done side, select a red that is mature and round.

International options: Red Burgundy, Oregon Pinot Noir, Barbaresco (Italy), red Rioja (Spain).

Canadian option: Ontario Pinot Noir or Merlot.

White wine option: Pouilly-Fumé.

HORSERADISH SAUCE

1/2 cup	sour cream	125 mL
1/4 cup	drained strong bottled horseradish	50 mL
1	apple, peeled and grated	1
Pinch	each granulated sugar, salt and pepper	Pinch

In small bowl, stir together sour cream, horseradish, apple, sugar, salt and pepper. Makes about 1 cup (250 mL).

This easy sauce can be made a few hours ahead, covered and refrigerated.

CELERY MASHED POTATOES

3 lb	potatoes (10 to 12)	1.5 kg
1/4 cup	butter	50 mL
6 cups	chopped celery and leaves	1.5 L
1	small onion, chopped	1
1/2 cup	light sour cream	125 mL
1/4 tsp	grated nutmeg	1 mL
	Salt and pepper	

Comforting mashed potatoes get a bit of texture and color from sautéed celery.

Peel and quarter potatoes. In saucepan of boiling salted water, cook potatoes until tender, about 20 minutes.

Meanwhile, in large skillet, melt butter over medium heat. Cook celery and onion, covered, for 10 minutes. Uncover and cook for 10 more minutes. Purée in food processor or blender.

Drain cooked potatoes well; return to low heat for about 1 minute to dry. Mash until smooth. Stir in celery mixture; gradually beat in sour cream, nutmeg, and salt and pepper to taste. (Potatoes can be cooled, covered and refrigerated for up to 1 day. Bring to room temperature before reheating, covered, in oven or microwave.) Makes 10 to 12 servings.

Brussels Sprouts Sautéed with Bacon

This simple treatment will convert anyone to being a Brussels sprouts lover. If you wish, for a more festive dish, toss in a couple of spoonfuls of diced red pepper when you reheat the sprouts.

2-1/2 lb	Brussels sprouts	1.25 kg
8	slices lean side bacon, diced	8
2 tbsp	white wine vinegar	25 mL
	Salt and pepper	

Trim Brussels sprouts; cut in two. Cook, uncovered, in large pot of boiling salted water for 5 minutes or until barely tender; drain well. (Sprouts can be prepared to this point, covered and left at room temperature for up to 4 hours.)

In large skillet, cook bacon over medium-high heat until crisp, stirring often. Toss in sprouts and vinegar; heat through. Season with salt and pepper to taste. Makes 12 servings.

Honey-Glazed Carrots and Parsnips

With a hint of curry, this easy make-ahead dish is the perfect accompaniment to a majestic roast of beef.

10	parsnips (about 2 lb/1 kg)	10
8	carrots (about 1-1/2 lb/750 g)	8
1/4 cup	butter	50 mL
1 cup	(approx) chicken stock	250 mL
	Salt and pepper	
1/4 cup	liquid honey	50 mL
4 tsp	fresh lemon juice	20 mL
2 tsp	curry powder	10 mL

Peel parsnips and carrots. Cut in half lengthwise; slice diagonally into 1/2-inch (1 cm) thick pieces.

In large skillet, combine carrots, butter, stock and pinch salt; bring to boil. Cover and reduce heat to medium; simmer for 4 minutes. Add parsnips and cook for 4 to 6 minutes or until vegetables are tender, adding a bit more stock if needed. With slotted spoon, transfer to shallow gratin dish. Sprinkle with salt and pepper to taste; let cool.

Meanwhile, add honey, lemon juice and curry powder to liquid in skillet; bring to boil. Boil for about 1 minute or until thickened. Cool and pour over vegetables. (Vegetables can be prepared to this point, covered and refrigerated for up to 1 day.)

Heat, uncovered, in 400°F (200°C) oven for 15 to 20 minutes or until lightly glazed and heated through, stirring once or twice. Makes 12 servings.

GREEN SALAD
WITH WALNUT DRESSING

2	heads Boston lettuce	2
1/2 cup	toasted walnut pieces	125 mL
Walnut Dressing:		
1/4 cup	walnut oil	50 mL
2 tbsp	olive oil	25 mL
2 tbsp	white wine vinegar	25 mL
2 tsp	Dijon mustard	10 mL
	Salt and pepper	

Walnut Dressing: Whisk together walnut oil, olive oil, vinegar, mustard, and salt and pepper to taste. (Dressing can be covered and refrigerated for up to 2 days; whisk before using.)

Tear lettuce into bite-sized pieces. Toss with walnuts and dressing in large salad bowl. Makes 12 small servings.

This simple salad will make only enough for a taste for twelve people — just perfect to refresh your guests before you bring on dessert.

Have the greens prepared, walnuts toasted and dressing made up to two days ahead so that it takes no more than five minutes to tear the greens and finish the salad to serve.

CRANBERRY CAKE WITH WHITE
CHOCOLATE GLAZE

2-2/3 cups	sifted cake-and-pastry flour	650 mL
1 tsp	baking soda	5 mL
1/2 tsp	salt	2 mL
3/4 cup	butter, at room temperature	175 mL
1-3/4 cups	granulated sugar	425 mL
3	eggs	3
1 tsp	vanilla	5 mL
1-1/4 cups	buttermilk	300 mL
1-1/2 cups	fresh or frozen cranberries,	375 mL
	patted dry and coarsely chopped	
3/4 cup	chopped pecans	175 mL
White Chocolate Glaze:		
12 oz	white chocolate, chopped	375 g
8 oz	cream cheese, at room temperature	250 g
1/4 cup	butter, at room temperature	50 mL
2 tbsp	kirsch	25 mL
1 tbsp	fresh lemon juice	15 mL
	Pecan halves	
	Dried cranberries (optional)	

Combine flour, baking soda and salt. In bowl, cream butter and sugar until light and fluffy. Beat in eggs, one at a time, beating well after each addition. Beat in vanilla. Add flour mixture in three

I love the zest of cranberries in baked things like cakes or muffins. Here, cranberries team up with pecans in a simple cake with an interesting icing. If you like, scoop a little ice cream alongside each piece. If using frozen berries, do not thaw.

additions alternately with two additions of buttermilk. Fold in cranberries and pecans.

Pour into three well-greased and floured 9-inch (1.5 L) round cake pans. Bake in 350°F (180°C) oven for about 25 minutes or until tester inserted into centre comes out clean. Cool in pans on racks for 10 minutes. Turn out onto racks to cool completely.

White Chocolate Glaze: Melt chocolate in double boiler set over hot water on low heat. (Do not have water too hot or have it touching bottom of upper pan.) Remove from heat; stir until smooth and cool.

In large bowl, beat cream cheese until smooth and creamy. Gradually beat in cooled chocolate, butter, kirsch and lemon juice. Chill just until firm enough to spread, about 20 minutes.

Spread thin layer of glaze on each cake layer. Assemble layers; spread glaze over top and sides. Decorate top with pecan halves, and dried cranberries if using. (Cake can be covered and refrigerated for up to 1 day.) Makes 12 servings.

THE WINE

White chocolate tastes sweeter than dark chocolate, but the tartness of the cranberries makes a refreshing contrast. High sugar and high acidity suggest one wine – Ontario Icewine. If this is unavailable, try a German Riesling of Beerenauslese quality.

SOPHISTICATED DINNER FOR FOUR

Mozzarella and Prosciutto Flowers

Herb-Roasted Salmon Steaks with Dill Cream

Tricolor Salad of Roasted Peppers

Steamed Snow Peas

Crisp Potato Roses

Walnut Bread

Cheese and Fresh Fruit

Sometimes I like to fuss just a little if I'm only having four at the table.

Although most of the other things take only minutes, the appetizer and potato side dish take a while to put together, but they're both very pretty and absolutely delicious...as is the Walnut Bread. If time runs out, you can always buy an interesting bread, but I find some people still like to bake their own, and this bread is certainly worth trying your hand at as an accompaniment to Brie or Stilton along with some pears and grapes.

PARTY PRIMER

1. *Up to six months ahead (if freezing) or one day ahead, make Walnut Bread.*
2. *Up to three days ahead, roast peppers and make Tricolor Salad.*
3. *One day ahead, marinate mozzarella.*
4. *One hour before baking, prepare Crisp Potato Roses.*
5. *Thirty minutes before serving, wrap mozzarella with prosciutto and arrange on plate. Trim snow peas. Bring salad to room temperature and toss with basil. Arrange cheese and fruit on serving plate.*
6. *Thirty minutes before roasting, prepare Herb-Roasted Salmon Steaks; prepare Dill Cream while steaks roast.*
7. *Steam snow peas.*

Mozzarella and Prosciutto Flowers

1	tangerine	1
1/4 cup	olive oil	50 mL
1	clove garlic, minced	1
2 tbsp	each chopped black olives and fresh parsley	25 mL
1/4 tsp	hot pepper flakes	1 mL
24	ciliegine (or 8 bocconcini, quartered)	24
8	thin slices prosciutto	8

Remove zest from tangerine and place in medium bowl. Squeeze tangerine juice over zest; stir in oil, garlic, olives, parsley and hot pepper flakes. Add cheese balls. Marinate, covered, overnight in refrigerator, stirring occasionally.

Cut prosciutto slices lengthwise into 3 strips each. Wrap 1 strip around each cheese ball and secure with toothpick if necessary. Makes 24 hors d'oeuvres.

One of my favorite quick appetizers is to wrap prosciutto around fruit — pear slices, melon balls, fresh fig wedges. This pretty variation is a taste-tempter using Italian soft cheese. You can buy fresh mozzarella, called ciliegine *or* bocconcini, *in Italian grocery stores. If unavailable, cut regular mozzarella into 1/2-inch (1 cm) cubes.*

THE WINE

Since you are going to have a fine white wine with the salmon, I suggest you extend the metaphor of sophistication by having a sparkling wine with this appetizer. Choose a Brut (the driest) sparkling wine to cleanse the palate of the saltiness of the prosciutto.

International option: Champagne Brut or Spanish Cava or German Sekt.
Canadian option: Canadian 'Champagne' Brut.

Herb-Roasted Salmon Steaks with Dill Cream

4	salmon steaks (about 1-inch/2.5 cm thick)	4
4 tsp	vegetable oil	20 mL
	Salt and pepper	
2 tbsp	chopped fresh parsley	25 mL
3 tbsp	snipped fresh dill	50 mL
2 tbsp	butter	25 mL
2	shallots, thinly sliced	2
1	clove garlic, minced	1
1/4 cup	dry white wine or fish stock	50 mL
1/4 cup	whipping cream	50 mL

Salmon steaks are the ultimate in fast, elegant fare. Here, a simple sauce, made while the steaks roast, is a good complement to their appearance and flavor.

Pat steaks dry and place in baking dish. Brush each with oil; sprinkle with salt and pepper, parsley and 1 tbsp (15 mL) of the dill. Let stand at room temperature for 30 minutes or refrigerate for up to 4 hours.

Roast in 450°F (230°C) oven for 10 minutes or until flesh just flakes when tested with fork.

Meanwhile, in small skillet, melt butter over medium heat; cook shallots and garlic, stirring constantly, for 3 minutes. Add remaining dill and wine; simmer for 1 minute. Stir in cream, and salt and pepper to taste; simmer until slightly thickened, about 2 minutes. Pour over fish and serve immediately. Makes 4 servings.

THE WINE

Salmon is the aristocrat of fish and calls for a fine white wine. The taste of dill marries well with oak-aged Chardonnay.

International option: White Burgundy, California Chardonnay or Australian Chardonnay.

Canadian option: Ontario or B.C. Chardonnay.

TRICOLOR SALAD OF ROASTED PEPPERS

3	sweet peppers	3
3 tbsp	olive oil	50 mL
2 tsp	white wine vinegar	10 mL
1	clove garlic, minced	1
	Salt and pepper	
1 tbsp	minced fresh basil	15 mL

Cut peppers into quarters and seed. Arrange skin side up on greased baking sheet. Brush generously with some of the oil; roast in 450°F (230°C) oven for about 15 minutes or until skins are blistered and charred. Remove from oven and place under overturned bowl to steam for 10 minutes. Peel and cut into strips. In bowl, stir together vinegar, garlic, salt and pepper to taste and remaining oil. Add peppers and toss to coat well. Let stand for at least 30 minutes at room temperature. (Salad can be covered and refrigerated for up to 3 days; bring to room temperature.) Toss with basil to serve. Makes 4 servings.

I love roasted peppers, but I hate separating the seeds from the rest of the soft peppers once they're peeled. For this reason, I tried quartering and seeding them before roasting, and it worked quite well to make this pretty salad quick and easy. Choose a combination of red, yellow and green or orange peppers.

CRISP POTATO ROSES

1/3 cup	unsalted butter	75 mL
1	small clove garlic, halved	1
1/2 tsp	each dried thyme and salt	2 mL
Pinch	each pepper and dried rosemary	Pinch
1-1/2 lb	small potatoes (about 6)	750 g

These lovely roses are composed of very thinly sliced potatoes arranged petallike in baking dishes. Use small potatoes, all about the same size.

In small saucepan, melt butter with garlic over low heat. Skim off any white solids and discard garlic. Brush four 3/4-cup (175 mL) custard cups or individual quiche pans with some of the butter. Stir thyme, salt, pepper and rosemary into remaining butter; set aside.

Peel potatoes; place in bowl of cold water. Drain and dry each potato as needed. With vegetable peeler or thin slicing blade of food processor, slice each potato as thinly as possible. As you work, add slices from each potato to butter mixture, tossing to coat well. Using slotted spoon, transfer slices in batches to big bowl.

Starting at edge of each prepared custard cup, overlap potato slices in circle. Arrange second overlapping circle on top about 1 inch (2.5 cm) from outer edge. Continue circles into centre. Dot with any remaining butter. (Potatoes can be prepared to this point and stand at room temperature for up to 1 hour.)

Bake in 450°F (230°C) oven for 30 to 40 minutes or until golden brown, crisp and tender when pierced in centre with fork. Makes 4 servings.

WALNUT BREAD

Pinch	granulated sugar	Pinch
1/2 cup	lukewarm water	125 mL
1	pkg active dry yeast (scant tbsp/15 mL)	1
3 cups	whole wheat flour	750 mL
3 cups	(approx) all-purpose flour	750 mL
2 tsp	salt	10 mL
2 cups	warm milk	500 mL
1/4 cup	walnut oil	50 mL
1/4 cup	finely ground walnuts	50 mL
1 tbsp	liquid honey	15 mL
1-1/2 cups	toasted walnut pieces	375 mL

Easy to make, this moist walnut bread will be a special treat for guests. Leftover bread is great toasted for breakfast or freezes well for another party. If you have a large mixer fitted with a dough hook, this is the time to use it.

In small bowl, dissolve sugar in water and sprinkle yeast on top; let stand until foamy and doubled in volume, about 10 minutes.

Meanwhile, in large bowl, combine whole wheat flour, I cup (250 mL) of the all-purpose flour and salt. Mix in milk, oil, ground walnuts and honey. Beat until smooth.

Stir yeast mixture and add to milk mixture; beat well for 5 minutes. Gradually beat in enough of the remaining flour to make soft dough. Beat in walnut pieces. Transfer to well-floured counter; knead for about 8 minutes or until smooth and elastic.

Shape into smooth ball and place in greased bowl, rotating dough to grease surface. Cover with greased waxed paper and damp cloth; let rise in warm place for about I hour or until doubled in volume. (Setting the bowl on a heating pad turned to low is an ideal warm place.)

Punch down dough and knead lightly. Divide into 3 portions. Form into oblong loaves and place in three greased 8-1/2 x 4-1/2-inch (1.5 L) loaf pans. Cover and let rise until almost doubled, about 45 minutes.

Bake in 350°F (180°C) oven for about 30 minutes or until loaves sound hollow when tapped on bottom. Remove to racks to cool. (Bread can be stored in airtight container for up to I day, or packaged in freezer bags and frozen for up to 6 months.) Makes 3 small loaves.

THE WINE

A glass of Oloroso sherry. Its nutty flavor will complement the bread and its sweetness will marry well with grapes and slices of pear.

Comforting Sunday Dinner For Six

Garlic-Roasted Chicken with Gravy

Creamy Mashed Potatoes

Steamed Green Beans

Orange-Roasted Beets

Buttermilk Coleslaw

Pear Crumble with Ginger Cream

*C*urrently very fashionable in bistro-style restaurants, this is the kind of old-fashioned meal that used to appear often on Sunday dinner tables. I especially remember the wonderful flavors of such a dinner on my family's farm where we raised our own plump chickens, fresh-from-the-garden vegetables and tree-ripened fruit.

If I wish to have an appetizer for this type of homey meal, I quite often go to our local deli for a nice slice of pâté. You might do the same for this menu, or instead of using the roasted garlic in the gravy, serve it with French bread and a fresh goat cheese as a sit-down first course.

The green beans are just steamed, then dressed with butter, salt, pepper, and lemon juice or vinegar if you wish.

PARTY PRIMER

1. *One day ahead, prepare Orange-Roasted Beets and Buttermilk Coleslaw.*
2. *Two hours before serving, prepare and roast chicken; then make gravy. Trim beans.*
3. *Thirty minutes before serving, peel and cook Creamy Mashed Potatoes. Reheat beets.*
4. *Prepare Pear Crumble to pop into oven as chicken comes out. Whip cream and refrigerate.*
5. *Steam beans.*

Garlic-Roasted Chicken with Gravy

1	roasting chicken (about 5 lb/2.5 kg)	1
Half	lemon	Half
	Salt and pepper	
2 tbsp	each butter and vegetable oil	25 mL
3	heads garlic (about 45 cloves)	3
1/2 tsp	each dried thyme and crushed dried sage	2 mL
1 cup	chicken stock	250 mL
1 tbsp	cornstarch	15 mL

Wipe chicken inside and out with damp cloth. Rub all over inside and out with lemon. Sprinkle inside with salt and pepper. Skewer neck skin to back and tie ends of legs together.

Melt butter with oil in roasting pan. Place chicken in pan and turn to coat all over with mixture; set to one side of pan.

Break garlic heads apart into cloves but do not peel; toss with remaining butter mixture in pan. Arrange chicken breast side up in pan; scatter garlic over top. Sprinkle with thyme, sage, salt and pepper. Roast, uncovered, in 350°F (180°C) oven for 1 hour and 30 to 45 minutes, brushing occasionally with pan juices, until chicken is golden brown, juices run clear when inner thigh is pierced and meat thermometer reaches 185°F (85°C). Remove to warm platter and keep warm.

Remove garlic from pan and set aside. Discard any fat from drippings. Place pan over high heat; add stock and bring to boil,

>>

The aroma of garlic cooking to mellow sweetness will envelope your whole house and coax hearty appetites for this succulent roast chicken. Guests can squeeze the soft pulp from the garlic's skin onto bread or into their mouths; or, squeeze it out before dinner, purée and add to the gravy. Either way, it's delicious!

THE WINE

This is one instance where the predominating interest is not in the meat but in the side dish – garlic. Since the emphasis is on family and comfort, the wine you choose is the wine everyone likes best, red or white. I would suggest a Sauvignon Blanc for white wine lovers and a Cabernet Sauvignon for red.

International option: White – Sonoma Sauvignon Blanc (California), New Zealand Sauvignon Blanc or Pouilly-Fumé from the Loire. Red – Cabernet Sauvignon from California, Australia or Chile.

Canadian option: White – Ontario Seyval Blanc, B.C. Chasselas. Red – Ontario Cabernet Sauvignon or Cabernet Franc.

stirring to scrape up any brown bits. Dissolve cornstarch in small amount of cold water; add to pan and cook, stirring, until thickened and bubbly. Season to taste with salt and pepper.

If adding garlic to gravy, pop centres into food processor or blender and purée. Stir into gravy and heat through. Or, just surround chicken on platter with cloves. Serve gravy in heated sauceboat. Makes 6 servings.

CREAMY MASHED POTATOES

The side dish that appeared at almost every supper around our farm's kitchen table while I was growing up has become upscale. The true comfort food of all time, mashed potatoes are currently appearing on all the best bistro menus.

6	potatoes	6
1/2 cup	warm whipping cream or milk	125 mL
1 tbsp	butter	15 mL
	Salt and pepper	

Peel and halve potatoes. In saucepan of boiling salted water, cook potatoes for about 20 minutes or until tender. Drain and return to low heat for about 2 minutes to dry.

Mash or put through ricer. With fork, gradually beat in warm cream and butter until fluffy. Season to taste with salt and pepper. Serve immediately. Makes 6 servings.

Note: Generally speaking, the long oblong baking potato is also good for mashing.

ORANGE-ROASTED BEETS

Roasting beets brings out their earthy flavor and aroma. The time varies a great deal with their age and size. The combination of orange and beets is always a magical one and a good accompaniment for chicken.

1-1/2 lb	small beets (about 12)	750 g
1 tbsp	olive oil	15 mL
1 tsp	grated orange zest	5 mL
1/4 cup	fresh orange juice	50 mL
Pinch	ground cloves	Pinch
	Salt and pepper	

Scrub beets and remove all but I inch (2.5 cm) of stems and tails. Place in shallow pan with 1/4 inch (5 mm) water. Cover with foil and bake in 375°F (190°C) oven for 35 to 50 minutes or until tender when pierced with knife. Drain; slip off skins and quarter.

In greased shallow baking dish, toss beets with oil, orange zest and juice, cloves, and salt and pepper to taste. (Beets can be prepared to this point, cooled, covered, and refrigerated for up to one day.)

Warm, covered, in 350°F (180°C) oven for I 5 to 25 minutes or until heated through. Makes 6 servings.

Buttermilk Coleslaw

Half	head green cabbage	Half
1 tsp	salt	5 mL
2/3 cup	each buttermilk and light mayonnaise	150 mL
1 tbsp	liquid honey	15 mL
1 tsp	dry mustard	5 mL
1	small red onion, finely diced	1
1 cup	grated carrot	250 mL
2 tbsp	chopped fresh parsley	25 mL
1 tbsp	snipped fresh dill	15 mL

Finely shred cabbage to make about 10 cups (2.5 L); place in bowl and toss with salt.

Stir together buttermilk, mayonnaise, honey and mustard; pour over cabbage. Stir in onion, carrot and half of the parsley. Cover and refrigerate for at least 12 hours or up to 24 hours.

Stir coleslaw; taste and adjust seasoning if necessary. To serve, sprinkle with remaining parsley and dill. Makes 6 to 8 servings.

The dressing is creamy but light in this simple coleslaw — always a favorite with roast chicken.

Pear Crumble with Ginger Cream

1/4 cup	dried currants	50 mL
2 tbsp	pear liqueur or kirsch	25 mL
2-1/2 lb	Bartlett pears (6 large)	1.25 kg
2 tbsp	fresh lemon juice	25 mL
1/2 cup	packed brown sugar	125 mL
1/2 cup	all-purpose flour	125 mL
1/2 cup	rolled oats	125 mL
1/2 cup	toasted chopped walnuts	125 mL
1 tsp	grated lemon zest	5 mL
1/4 tsp	each salt, ground cinnamon and grated nutmeg	1 mL
1/4 cup	butter	50 mL
Ginger Cream:		
1 cup	whipping cream	250 mL
2 tbsp	icing sugar	25 mL
4 tsp	minced candied ginger	20 mL

Combine currants with liqueur; set aside. Peel, core and thinly slice pears. Place in large bowl; stir in lemon juice, half of the brown sugar and 2 tbsp (25 mL) of the flour.

In separate bowl, stir together remaining sugar, remaining flour, oats, walnuts, lemon zest, salt, cinnamon and nutmeg; cut in butter until crumbly.

Juicy baked pear slices with a crisp topping and spicy cream accompaniment make an inviting, soothing finale to any meal.

Stir currants and liqueur into pears; spread in greased shallow 8-cup (2 L) baking or gratin dish. Sprinkle with oat mixture. Bake in 375°F (190°C) oven for 40 to 45 minutes or until crumble begins to brown on top and pears are tender.

Ginger Cream: Meanwhile whip cream and icing sugar together until soft peaks form; fold in ginger. Serve alongside warm crumble. Makes 6 to 8 servings.

THE WINE

Certain sweet Muscats have an almost gingery character that would complement the flavor of the cream while allowing the pear's gentle acidity to express itself.

International option: Muscat de Beaumes de Venise (France) or sweet Malvasia (Italy).

Canadian option: Late Harvest Riesling.

FRIDAY NIGHT FIRESIDE SUPPER FOR FOUR

Sage Leaf Focaccia

Spicy Lamb Sausage Patties

Winter Tomato Pudding

*Orange and Onion Salad
with Olive and Lemon Vinaigrette*

Hot Fudge Cappuccino Sundaes

$\mathcal{E}$asy to serve and eat, this is the type of meal that's fun to 'cosy-down' with in front of a fire.

You might serve the simple Focaccia along with the Sausage Patties and Tomato Pudding; or, serve it as an appetizer and pass some whole grain rolls with the main course.

If time runs out, cheat and buy a good coffee ice cream for the sundaes.

PARTY PRIMER

1. *Up to two months ahead, make and freeze pizza dough for Sage Leaf Focaccia.*
2. *Up to one week ahead, prepare chocolate sauce for sundaes.*
3. *One day ahead, prepare Spicy Lamb Sausage Patties. Make cappuccino ice cream.*
4. *Several hours ahead, prepare tomato and crumb mixture for Winter Tomato Pudding.*
5. *About one hour before serving focaccia, soak sage leaves; make focaccia.*
6. *Two hours before serving, make Orange and Onion Salad.*
7. *About 45 minutes before serving, assemble and bake tomato pudding.*
8. *Cook patties.*
9. *Just before serving, make sundaes.*

Sage Leaf Focaccia

24	small fresh or dried whole sage leaves	24
2 tbsp	olive oil	25 mL
	Pizza Dough (recipe, page 74)	
3/4 cup	freshly grated Parmesan cheese	175 mL
	Cornmeal	
	Coarse salt and pepper	

Soak sage leaves in olive oil for at least 30 minutes.

Meanwhile, punch dough down and knead in 1/4 cup (50 mL) of the cheese. Roll out into 12-inch (30 cm) circle and place on cornmeal-sprinkled pizza pan. Sprinkle with sage mixture, salt and pepper to taste, and remaining cheese.

Bake in 425°F (220°C) oven for 20 to 25 minutes or until golden. Cut into wedges to serve warm. Makes 4 servings.

This absolutely delicious flatbread can be made in no time with pizza dough available in most grocery stores. Or just go into any pizza parlor and ask for enough for one crust. But making your own dough is satisfying and so easy that you probably won't want to make the trip to the store.

Spicy Lamb Sausage Patties

1-1/4 lb	trimmed lean lamb (shoulder or leg)	625 g
1 cup	pecan halves	250 mL
1 tbsp	minced fresh ginger	15 mL
1 tsp	grated orange zest	5 mL
1 tsp	salt	5 mL
1/2 tsp	pepper	2 mL
1/2 tsp	each crumbled dried rosemary and thyme	2 mL
1/4 tsp	hot pepper flakes	1 mL
2 tbsp	vegetable oil	25 mL

Cut lamb into 1-inch (2.5 cm) cubes. Grind about 1 cup (250 mL) at a time in food processor or meat grinder; do not overprocess. Remove to big bowl.

Chop pecans very finely in food processor; add to meat along with ginger, orange zest, salt, pepper, rosemary, thyme and hot pepper flakes. Combine gently but don't overmix; refrigerate until chilled. Test for seasoning by frying tiny ball of sausage mixture in a little oil until no longer pink inside; taste and adjust seasoning of meat mixture in bowl if desired.

With moist hands and using 1/2 cup (125 mL) mixture for each patty, gently form into 3-inch (8 cm) rounds. (Patties can be placed in single layer on plate, covered and refrigerated overnight.)

In large skillet, heat oil over medium-high heat; fry chilled patties for about 8 minutes, turning once, or until no longer pink inside. Makes 8 patties.

For these interesting and tasty homemade sausage patties, be sure to buy enough meat to have sufficient for the recipe after the lamb is trimmed. All fat and gristle have to be removed.

WINTER TOMATO PUDDING

A kind of stewed tomato casserole, this comforting hot dish goes particularly well with the spicy sausage patties. Although it can't be made ahead, you can prepare the crumbs and the tomato mixture early in the day to layer just before baking.

2 tbsp	vegetable or olive oil	25 mL
1	clove garlic, crushed	1
2 cups	coarse fresh bread crumbs	500 mL
1/4 cup	chopped fresh parsley	50 mL
2 tbsp	butter	25 mL
1/4 cup	chopped shallots	50 mL
3 tbsp	packed brown sugar	50 mL
1 tsp	dried marjoram	5 mL
1/2 tsp	salt	2 mL
1/4 tsp	pepper	1 mL
1	can (28 oz/796 mL) tomatoes (undrained), chopped	1
1	can (5-1/2 oz/156 mL) tomato paste	1

In large skillet, heat oil over low heat; cook garlic for 3 minutes. Add bread crumbs and parsley; cook over medium heat until brown and crisp, about 5 minutes. Remove from pan and set aside.

Melt butter in skillet over medium-low heat; cook shallots for 3 minutes. Stir in brown sugar, marjoram, salt and pepper until well combined. Stir in tomatoes and paste.

Spoon half of the mixture into greased 8-cup (2 L) baking dish; top with half of the bread crumb mixture. Repeat layers. Bake, uncovered, in 350°F (180°C) oven for 35 to 40 minutes or until thickened and bubbling. Serve warm. Makes 4 servings.

THE WINE

This medley of dishes offers a tempting range of flavors and requires a wine of great character to accompany them. Since the dominant theme is Italian, I would suggest a fine Italian white wine with an elegant dry, herby flavor. You could, however, choose a light Italian red such as Grignolino or Dolcetto, both with good acidity.

International option: Vernaccia di San Gimignano or Oregon Pinot Gris.

Canadian option: B.C. Pinot Blanc.

Orange and Onion Salad with Olive and Lemon Vinaigrette

3	navel oranges, preferably blood	3
1	small red onion	1
1/4 cup	oil-cured olives	50 mL
Pinch	hot pepper flakes	Pinch
	Salt and coarsely ground pepper	
2 tbsp	olive oil	25 mL
1 tbsp	fresh lemon juice	15 mL
	Chopped fresh basil or parsley	

Using sharp knife, peel oranges, removing all white pith. Slice crosswise into 1/4-inch (5 mm) thick slices. Arrange on large platter. Very thinly slice onion crosswise and separate into rings; scatter over oranges.

Halve and pit olives; scatter over onions. Sprinkle with hot pepper flakes; season with salt and generously with pepper. Drizzle with oil and lemon juice; sprinkle with basil. Cover with plastic wrap and let stand at room temperature for about 2 hours before serving. Makes 4 servings.

The Wine

I would avoid any wine with this salad as the orange and lemon would gang up on anything you tried to match.

I love the mix of tangy citrus flavors and sprightly onion taste in this traditional Sicilian winter salad. Two other reasons also make this appealing: it takes only minutes to make and is best served at room temperature. If you happen to find blood oranges, switch the onion to a white one.

Hot Fudge Cappuccino Sundaes

4 tsp	espresso granules	20 mL
1 tsp	ground cinnamon	5 mL
1/4 tsp	ground cardamom	1 mL
2 cups	light cream	500 mL
1/2 cup	(approx) granulated sugar	125 mL
1/2 cup	freshly brewed espresso, cooled	125 mL
1/2 cup	hazelnuts	125 mL
1 tbsp	Frangelico liqueur	15 mL
	Dark Chocolate Sauce (recipe follows)	

This sophisticated version of the good old-fashioned hot fudge sundae is perfect for company.

In small heavy saucepan, stir together espresso granules, cinnamon and cardamom; blend in cream and sugar. Over medium heat, bring to foaming near-boil, stirring to dissolve sugar; remove from heat. Cover tightly and let stand for at least 30 minutes or until cool.

Line small sieve with several layers of rinsed cheesecloth; set over bowl. Strain mixture, pressing and scraping bottom of sieve to extract all liquid. Stir brewed espresso into bowl. Add more sugar if desired. Freeze in ice-cream maker according to manufacturer's instructions.

Meanwhile, spread hazelnuts on baking sheet; toast in 350°F (180°C) oven for about 5 minutes or until fragrant. Enclose in clean tea towel and rub briskly to remove most of the skins. Chop coarsely, if desired.

Stir Frangelico into warm Dark Chocolate Sauce. To serve, scoop cappuccino ice cream into dishes. Drizzle with sauce; sprinkle with hazelnuts. Makes about 4 sundaes.

Dark Chocolate Sauce:

1/4 cup	whipping cream	50 mL
5 oz	bittersweet or semisweet chocolate, coarsely chopped	150 g
1 tbsp	butter	15 mL

In small heavy-bottomed saucepan, bring cream to boil over high heat; remove from heat. Stir in chocolate until melted; stir in butter. Let cool slightly before using. (Sauce can be covered and refrigerated for up to 1 week; warm over low heat.) Makes 1 cup (250 mL).

THE WINE

Two of the most difficult tastes to match with wine are chocolate and coffee. This recipe calls for both (Thanks, Rose!). If you want to have an accompanying beverage, pour small glasses of Frangelico.

Fireside Supper for Eight

Mushroom and Swiss Cheese Strudel

Osso Buco-Style Braised Lamb

*Orzo or Rice Spiced with Saffron, Parsley
and Olive Oil*

Buttered Rolls

*Salad of Mixed Greens
with Orange-Rosemary Vinaigrette*

Cappuccino Mousse Cake

*A*lmost completely make-ahead, this delicious fork supper is the kind of meal I love to serve when winter winds are blowing and I want warm conversation around the fire.

The delicious stew is a lamb version of a popular veal dish, and is perfectly complemented by the flavors suggested for the orzo and the zesty salad dressing.

PARTY PRIMER

1. *Two months or two days ahead, make and freeze or refrigerate Braised Lamb.*
2. *One month or two days ahead, make and freeze or refrigerate Cappuccino Mousse Cake.*
3. *Two days ahead, assemble Strudel.*
4. *One day ahead, wash and dry salad greens; make vinaigrette.*
5. *Several hours ahead, make Gremolata for lamb.*
6. *Up to two hours ahead, tear greens for salad and toss with sliced onion.*
7. *Thirty minutes before serving, bake Strudel.*
8. *Reheat Braised Lamb.*
9. *Cook orzo and stir in saffron, chopped parsley and olive oil.*
10. *Just before mealtime, garnish cake with whipped cream and shaved chocolate.*
11. *Just before serving, toss salad with dressing.*

MUSHROOM AND SWISS CHEESE STRUDEL

2 tbsp	olive oil	25 mL
1	onion, chopped	1
2	cloves garlic, minced	2
1	sweet red pepper, diced	1
1 lb	mushrooms, sliced	500 g
1/2 tsp	each dried thyme, marjoram and oregano	2 mL
	Salt and pepper	
8	sheets phyllo pastry	8
1/2 cup	butter, melted (preferably unsalted)	125 mL
1/2 cup	dry bread crumbs	125 mL
2 cups	shredded Swiss cheese	500 mL

Tucked away in the refrigerator, this hearty appetizer just needs a few minutes in the oven before serving.

In large skillet, heat oil over medium heat; cook onion, garlic and red pepper for 5 minutes. Add mushrooms, thyme, marjoram, oregano, and salt and pepper to taste. Increase heat to high and cook, stirring often, for 3 to 5 minutes or until liquid has evaporated. Cool.

Lightly dampen tea towel. Lay 1 sheet of phyllo on towel. Brush with melted butter; sprinkle lightly with bread crumbs. Repeat layering with 3 more sheets.

With slotted spoon, arrange half of the mushroom mixture in strip along narrow end, leaving 2-inch (5 cm) border uncovered at end and sides. Sprinkle half of the cheese over mushroom mixture. Starting at filling end, roll up pastry part way; fold in sides and roll up completely to enclose filling. Place seam side down on buttered baking sheet. Brush top with butter. Repeat with remaining phyllo and filling. (Strudel can be prepared to this point, covered and refrigerated for up to 2 days.)

Cut 7 slits in top of each roll. Bake in 400°F (200°C) oven for 25 to 30 minutes or until golden brown. Slice to serve. Makes 8 servings.

THE WINE

Eight people is an ideal number if you intend to have more than one bottle of wine, since you can pour a moderate glass for each guest from a single bottle.

The buttery pastry combined with the cheese in the Strudel calls for a hefty, oak-aged Chardonnay.

International option: Australian or Californian Chardonnay.

Canadian option: B.C. or Ontario barrel-fermented Chardonnay.

OSSO BUCO-STYLE BRAISED LAMB

Long cooking makes this lamb fork-tender. Having it sit at least overnight will develop even more flavor. Serve with orzo spiced with a pinch of saffron, some chopped parsley and a drizzle of olive oil.

2 tbsp	butter	25 mL
1	onion, finely chopped	1
2	each carrots and stalks celery, diced	2
2	cloves garlic, minced	2
2	strips (4 inches/10 cm each) lemon peel	2
3 to 4 lb	boneless lamb shoulder (2 shoulders)	1.5 to 2 kg
1/2 cup	all-purpose flour	125 mL
	Salt and pepper	
3 tbsp	olive oil	50 mL
1 cup	dry white wine	250 mL
1-1/2 cups	chicken stock	375 mL
1-1/2 cups	plum tomatoes (undrained), coarsely chopped	375 mL
3	sprigs parsley	3
2	bay leaves	2
Gremolata:		
2	cloves garlic, minced	2
2 tbsp	minced fresh parsley	25 mL
1 tbsp	chopped lemon zest	15 mL

In large ovenproof saucepan or flameproof casserole, melt butter over medium heat; cook onion, carrots and celery for 10 minutes, stirring often. Add garlic and lemon peel; remove from heat and set aside.

Trim off any fat from lamb; cut into 2-inch (5 cm) cubes and pat dry. On plate, combine flour and 1/4 tsp (1 mL) each salt and pepper; dredge lamb in flour. In large skillet, heat oil over medium-high heat; brown lamb on all sides in batches, removing to place on vegetables in saucepan.

Pour off any fat from skillet. Add wine and boil for 3 minutes, scraping up any brown bits. Pour over lamb. Add stock to skillet and bring to simmer; add tomatoes, parsley, bay leaves, and salt and pepper to taste. Pour over lamb.

Bring lamb mixture to boil on top of stove. Cover tightly and bake in 350°F (180°C) oven for 2 hours. Discard lemon peel, parsley sprigs and bay leaves. (Lamb can be cooled, covered and refrigerated for up to 2 days or frozen for up to 2 months; thaw if frozen and heat in 350°F/180°C oven for 30 to 40 minutes or until heated through. Or, bring to simmer over medium-high heat; reduce heat and simmer, covered, for 5 minutes.)

Gremolata: Combine garlic, parsley and lemon zest. Sprinkle over stew 5 to 10 minutes before removing from oven to serve. Makes 8 servings.

┌─────────────────────────────┐

THE WINE

The conventional wisdom suggests Cabernet Sauvignon with lamb, but the addition of tomatoes and other vegetables adds acidity to the dish. I would look to an Italian red which would be more in keeping with the style of preparation.

International option: Chianti Classico Riserva, Barbaresco or Californian Sangiovese.

Canadian option: Ontario Maréchal Foch.

White wine option: Australian or Californian Chardonnay.

└─────────────────────────────┘

SALAD OF MIXED GREENS WITH ORANGE-ROSEMARY VINAIGRETTE

16 cups	torn assorted salad greens (watercress, leaf lettuce, Boston lettuce, Belgian endive, romaine)	4 L
1	small red onion, thinly sliced	1
Orange-Rosemary Vinaigrette:		
1/4 cup	fresh orange juice	50 mL
2 tbsp	white wine vinegar	25 mL
2 tsp	Dijon mustard	10 mL
1 tsp	crumbled dried rosemary	5 mL
1/2 tsp	finely grated orange zest	2 mL
1/3 cup	olive oil	75 mL
	Salt and pepper	

Dress a simple green salad with an interesting vinaigrette that can be made a day ahead. Its flavors complement the lamb perfectly.

Orange-Rosemary Vinaigrette: In small bowl, whisk together orange juice, vinegar, mustard, rosemary and orange zest; gradually whisk in oil. Season with salt and pepper to taste. (Dressing can be covered and refrigerated for up to 1 day.)

In salad bowl, toss greens and onion together. (Can be covered with tea towel and refrigerated for up to 2 hours.) Just before serving, pour on dressing and toss to coat. Makes 8 servings.

CAPPUCCINO MOUSSE CAKE

4 oz	hazelnuts	125 g
2 tbsp	butter, melted	25 mL
12 oz	semisweet chocolate, coarsely chopped	375 g
1/4 cup	instant espresso granules or other dry instant coffee	50 mL

Easy but decadent, this moist cake is a fabulous make-ahead dessert that needs only a last-minute garnishing flourish.

3/4 cup	whipping cream	175 mL
5	eggs	5
1 tsp	vanilla	5 mL
1/4 cup	each all-purpose flour and granulated sugar	50 mL

Garnish:

1 cup	whipping cream	250 mL
1 tbsp	icing sugar	15 mL
1 tsp	espresso granules	5 mL
	Shaved chocolate	

Spread hazelnuts on baking sheet; toast in 350°F (180°C) oven for about 5 minutes or until fragrant. Enclose in clean tea towel and rub briskly to remove most of the skins. Chop finely and combine with butter. Press onto bottom of greased 8-inch (2 L) springform pan. Set aside.

In saucepan, combine chocolate and coffee powder with half the cream; stir over low heat until chocolate is melted. Remove from heat.

In large bowl, beat eggs and vanilla on low speed until well mixed. Add flour and sugar; beat until thick and lemon colored, about 10 minutes.

Whip remaining cream until soft peaks form. Stir one-quarter of the egg mixture into chocolate. Fold in remainder; then whipped cream. Turn into prepared pan. Set pan in bigger pan containing enough boiling water to come halfway up sides of pans. Bake in 350°F (180°C) oven for about 1 hour or until top is dry. Cool 20 minutes; remove sides of pan. Cool completely. (Edges will be sticky.) Refrigerate in airtight container at least overnight or for up to 2 days or freeze for up to 2 months.

Garnish: To serve, whip cream with sugar and espresso granules; spread thin layer over top of cake. Pipe remainder in spiral pattern toward middle of cake. Sprinkle with shaved chocolate. Makes 8 to 10 servings.

THE WINE

To match the weight of this dessert, you would need a fortified wine or a chocolate/coffee cream liqueur (such as Bailey's or Devonshire Cream).

International option: Sweet Oloroso Sherry or the orange-flavored Quady Essensia from California.

Canadian option: Cream Sherry.

Tapas Supper for Six or More

Garlic Shrimp

Crusty Bread

Spicy Chorizo Slices with Orange

Roasted Red Peppers in Vinaigrette

Assorted Olives

White Bean Salad

Marinated Mussels

Spanish Onion and Potato Omelet

Fresh Fruit

*T*apas describes the delicious little dishes that are eaten in Spain at bars and taverns before lunch and dinner. Becoming popular here, they are replacing our old-fashioned cocktail party fare which left you too full to enjoy dinner and not satisfied enough to dispense with the evening meal.

Much more fun than the traditional cocktail party too, a sampling of zesty little bites can become a casual party that might be a co-operative project for close friends. In any event, the dishes that follow are simple and easy enough if you want to do them all yourself. They can be supplemented by purchased treats like olives and bread, and if you wish to make it into a real meal, finish with some nice fresh fruit.

PARTY PRIMER

1. *Up to three days ahead, prepare Roasted Red Peppers in Vinaigrette.*
2. *One day ahead, cook and marinate Mussels.*
3. *Several hours ahead, prepare Chorizo Slices and White Bean Salad.*
4. *Two or three hours ahead, prepare Potato Omelet.*
5. *A few minutes before cooking, prepare and salt Garlic Shrimp.*
6. *Just before serving, arrange mussels in shells.*
7. *Cook shrimp.*

Garlic Shrimp

1 lb	fresh medium shrimp, shelled and deveined	500 g
	Coarse salt	
1/3 cup	olive oil	75 mL
4	cloves garlic, chopped	4
1/4 tsp	hot pepper flakes	1 mL
1/2 tsp	paprika	2 mL
1 tsp	fresh lemon juice	5 mL
2 tbsp	chopped fresh parsley	25 mL

Dry shrimp well and sprinkle lightly with salt on both sides. Let stand at room temperature for 10 minutes.

In large skillet, heat oil over medium-high heat. Add shrimp in one layer; sprinkle with garlic and hot pepper flakes. Cook, stirring, for about 2 minutes or just until shrimp turn pink and are firm. Do not overcook. Stir in paprika, then lemon juice and parsley. Serve immediately. Makes 4 to 6 servings.

Pass lots of crusty bread to mop up all the wonderful juices from this garlicky dish.

Spicy Chorizo Slices with Orange

1 lb	chorizo sausages	500 g
1 tbsp	olive oil	15 mL
1	clove garlic, minced	1
2 tbsp	dry white wine or orange juice	25 mL
1 tsp	grated orange zest	5 mL

Slice chorizo into 1/4-inch (5 mm) thick slices. In skillet, heat oil over medium heat; cook garlic until golden.

Add chorizo and brown on both sides. Stir in wine and orange zest; simmer until wine has evaporated. Serve hot or cold. Makes about 6 servings.

For these spicy little nibbles, you might like to parboil the slices if the chorizo is particularly salty. Dry well before sautéing.

ROASTED RED PEPPERS IN VINAIGRETTE

The rich smoky flavor of these bright peppers is worth the time it takes to peel and seed them.

3	large sweet red peppers	3
1/2 tsp	paprika	2 mL
1/3 cup	olive oil	75 mL
2 tbsp	red wine vinegar	25 mL
Pinch	dried thyme	Pinch
2	cloves garlic, minced	2
	Salt and pepper	

Roast peppers under broiler, on grill, or in 450°F (230°C) oven for about 15 minutes, turning often, until blistered and charred all over. Remove and place under overturned bowl to steam for 10 minutes. Peel, seed and cut into 1/2-inch (1 cm) wide strips.

In bowl, dissolve paprika in 1 tbsp (15 mL) water. Stir in oil, vinegar, thyme, garlic, and salt and pepper to taste. Add pepper strips and marinate, refrigerated, for up to 3 days. Bring to room temperature to serve. Makes 4 to 6 servings.

WHITE BEAN SALAD

Simple and quick to make, this is sure to be a winner.

1	can (19 oz/540 mL) white pea (navy) beans	1
2 tbsp	olive oil	25 mL
2	hard-cooked egg yolks	2
2 tbsp	chopped onion	25 mL
1 tbsp	white wine vinegar	15 mL
1	clove garlic	1
1	tomato, diced	1
4	black olives, coarsely chopped	4
	Chopped fresh parsley	
	Salt and pepper	

Drain beans and rinse under cold running water; drain well again and place in medium bowl.

In food processor, purée olive oil, egg yolks, onion and vinegar, dropping garlic through feed tube with motor running. Toss with beans.

Add tomato, olives and 1 tbsp (15 mL) chopped parsley; gently combine. Season to taste with salt and pepper. Cover and let stand at room temperature for 1 hour. Or refrigerate for up to 4 hours; bring to room temperature to serve. Sprinkle with more parsley. Makes 4 to 6 servings.

Marinated Mussels

2 lb	mussels (about 40)	1 kg
1/4 cup	chopped onion	50 mL
1	lemon, cut in wedges	1
1/4 cup	olive oil	50 mL
3	cloves garlic, minced	3
3 tbsp	red wine vinegar	50 mL
2 tbsp	chopped fresh parsley	25 mL
1 tbsp	minced sweet red pepper	15 mL
2 tsp	small capers	10 mL
1/2 tsp	each paprika and grated lemon zest	2 mL
	Salt and pepper	

Wonderfully tangy and fresh tasting, these colorful mussels will become a favorite appetizer to serve at regular dinner parties. For the best flavor, be sure to make them a day ahead.

Scrub mussels well, removing beards. Discard any that do not close tightly.

In large saucepan, bring 1/2 cup (125 mL) water, onion and 1 lemon wedge to simmer. Add mussels; cover and steam until mussels open, about 5 minutes. Discard any that do not open. Using slotted spoon, transfer mussels to plate. Boil cooking liquid for about 3 minutes to reduce to 1/2 cup (125 mL). Remove lemon wedge.

In large skillet, heat oil over medium heat; cook garlic for 2 minutes. Add mussel liquid, vinegar, parsley, red pepper, capers, paprika, lemon zest, and salt and pepper to taste. Pour into medium bowl. Remove mussels from shells and add to bowl, reserving one half of each shell in refrigerator. Cover mussels and refrigerate for at least 2 hours or preferably 24 hours.

To serve, arrange mussel shells on platter. Place one mussel on each shell. Pour marinade over top. Garnish with remaining lemon wedges. Makes 6 servings.

SPANISH ONION AND POTATO OMELET (TORTILLA A LA ESPANOLA)

A tapas classic, this egg-bound potato pancake is good hot or made ahead and served at room temperature.

1/2 cup	olive oil	125 mL
4	large potatoes, peeled and thinly sliced	4
	Salt and pepper	
1	big Spanish onion, chopped	1
1	clove garlic, minced	1
6	eggs	6

In large ovenproof skillet, heat oil over medium-high heat. Sprinkle potatoes with salt and pepper; fry, in 2 batches; and turning occasionally with spatula, until golden brown on both sides. Transfer to paper-towel-lined bowl to drain.

Drain off all but 2 tbsp (25 mL) oil from skillet; cook onion and garlic over low heat for 20 minutes without browning, stirring often. Remove from heat and layer potato slices on top.

In small bowl, beat eggs with 1/2 tsp (2 mL) salt and 1/4 tsp (1 mL) pepper; pour over potatoes. Return skillet to medium heat; cook, shaking pan to prevent sticking, until bottom and sides are set, 4 to 5 minutes.

Run knife around edge to release sides; broil for 2 minutes to finish cooking top. Run metal spatula all around sides and as far under omelet as possible. Invert big plate over top and turn upside down to turn out omelet. Cut into wedges to serve hot or at room temperature. Makes 6 to 8 servings.

THE WINE

Do what the Spanish do. Have well-chilled bottles of Fino or Manzanilla sherry in coolers on the table and serve it in *copitas* — small chimney-shaped glasses. The crispness of the sherry cuts through the saltiness of the shrimp, mussels and olives, the spicy taste of the sausage and the roasted flavor of the red peppers.

If you prefer wine to sherry, try a Muscadet (Loire) or Aligoté (Burgundy or Ontario), Quincy or Menetou-Salon (Loire), Fendant (Switzerland) — something very dry. To be authentic, a white from Spain's Penedes or Rioja regions.

Canadian option: B.C. dry Riesling or Ontario Auxerrois.

Chalet Supper for Eight

Tortilla Chips

Peppery Sausage and Chicken Stew

Cheddar Cornbread

Mixed Salad Greens with Citrus Dressing

Apricot-Rum Pound Cake

When you head off to the ski slopes for a winter weekend of outdoor fun, it's always enjoyable to have friends share the time with you. Since fresh air produces good appetites, be prepared with this hearty menu that is easy to prepare and transport.

PARTY PRIMER

1. *Two months or up to three days ahead, make and freeze or refrigerate cake.*
2. *Up to two days ahead, make Chicken Stew. Make Citrus Dressing for salad; wash and dry greens and wrap well.*
3. *Up to one day ahead, make Tortilla Chips if serving cold; or, grate cheese, measure ingredients and carry to chalet if serving them hot. Measure out dry ingredients for Cheddar Cornbread to carry in plastic bag.*
4. *Just before mealtime, reheat stew. Bake Cornbread.*
5. *Make Tortilla Chips if serving hot.*
6. *Toss salad with dressing.*

TORTILLA CHIPS

6	8-inch (20 cm) flour tortillas	6
	Vegetable oil	
2 tsp	chili powder	10 mL
1/2 tsp	each salt, dried oregano and ground cumin	2 mL
1-1/2 cups	shredded Monterey Jack or mild Cheddar cheese	375 mL

Brush top of tortillas lightly with oil. Combine chili powder, salt, oregano and cumin; sprinkle over tortillas. Evenly sprinkle cheese on top.

With sharp knife, cut each tortilla into 15 thin wedges. Arrange on baking sheet and bake in 375°F (190°C) oven for about 5 minutes or until crisp and golden. Makes 90 pieces.

These easy homemade chips can be made ahead and served cold or eaten while hot from the oven. Either way, they'll disappear quickly.

THE WINE

The accent is on spices in this portable meal so choose gutsy whites and down-home reds to add to the Rocky Mountain feeling.

The chili powder and cumin in the Tortilla Chips will play havoc with anything delicate. You need a solid artisanal dry white with good acidity.

International option: Portuguese or Spanish white, Soave (Italy), white Rhône, Alsatian Edelzwicker.

Canadian option: Ontario Seyval, Quebec Seyval, B.C. Auxerrois.

PEPPERY SAUSAGE AND CHICKEN STEW

8	chicken legs (about 4 lb/2 kg)	8
1 tsp	each dried oregano, dry mustard and dried marjoram	5 mL
1/2 tsp	each salt, pepper and ground cumin	2 mL
1/4 tsp	cayenne pepper	1 mL
2 tbsp	olive oil	25 mL
1-1/2 lb	chorizo, Italian or other spicy fresh sausage, thinly sliced	750 g
12	cloves garlic, halved	12
4	carrots, cut in large chunks	4
2	onions, sliced	2

This colorful chicken stew will be a hit with everyone, including the cook, since it is even better if made one day and reheated another. Use a large chicken, cut up, or your favorite pieces like drumsticks and thighs.

2	sweet red or yellow peppers (or combination), cut in thin strips	2
1	jalapeño pepper, seeded and diced	1
1	can (28 oz/796 mL) Italian plum tomatoes, drained and quartered	1
1/4 cup	chopped fresh parsley or coriander	50 mL

Wipe chicken with damp cloth. Stir together oregano, mustard, marjoram, salt, pepper, cumin and cayenne; rub over chicken pieces. Refrigerate, covered, in large bowl for I hour.

In large skillet, heat oil over medium-high heat; brown sausages well, about 10 minutes. With slotted spoon, remove to drain on paper towels. Pour off all but 2 tbsp (25 mL) drippings in skillet; brown chicken, in batches, and transfer to large shallow casserole.

Discard all but 2 tbsp (25 mL) drippings in skillet; cook garlic, carrots and onions, covered, over medium heat for about 7 minutes, stirring occasionally, or until carrots are slightly tender. Add sweet and jalapeño peppers; cook for 2 minutes. Arrange vegetables and sausages around chicken pieces. Add tomatoes to skillet and bring to boil, scraping up any brown bits; pour over chicken.

Bake, covered and basting often with juices, in 400°F (200°C) oven for 45 to 50 minutes or until juices run clear when thickest part of chicken thigh is pierced or until chicken is no longer pink near bone. (Stew can be cooled, covered and refrigerated for up to 2 days; reheat in 350°F/180°C oven for 30 to 40 minutes.) Sprinkle with parsley to serve. Makes 8 generous servings.

THE WINE

Again the emphasis in the stew is on the hot spices. You'll need a red with lots of power.

International option: Portuguese red, Zinfandel (California), Barolo (Italy), Côtes du Rhône, Hungarian/Bulgarian reds.

Canadian option: Ontario Maréchal Foch.

CHEDDAR CORNBREAD

1-1/4 cups	cornmeal	300 mL
1 cup	shredded old Cheddar cheese	250 mL
3/4 cup	all-purpose flour	175 mL
1 tbsp	baking powder	15 mL
1/4 tsp	salt	1 mL
2	eggs	2
3/4 cup	milk	175 mL
1/3 cup	vegetable oil	75 mL
1	can (7 oz/199 mL) whole kernel corn, drained	1
2 tbsp	snipped fresh chives	25 mL

In large bowl, stir together cornmeal, cheese, flour, baking powder and salt.

Whisk together eggs, milk and oil; stir into dry ingredients just until blended. Stir in corn and chives; spoon into greased 8-inch (2 L) square cake pan. Bake in 400°F (200°C) oven for about 35 minutes or until tester inserted in centre comes out clean. Makes 8 generous servings.

Everyone likes cornbread, and nothing is better than this quick and easy cheesy version.

MIXED SALAD GREENS WITH CITRUS DRESSING

16 cups	torn mixed salad greens	4 L
6	mushrooms, sliced	6
Half	red onion, thinly sliced	Half
1	avocado, peeled and sliced	1
Citrus Dressing:		
1/3 cup	fresh orange juice	75 mL
1/4 cup	fresh lemon juice	50 mL
2 tbsp	olive oil	25 mL
1	green onion, minced	1
1	clove garlic, minced	1
1/2 tsp	salt	2 mL
1/4 tsp	pepper	1 mL
Pinch	each granulated sugar, hot pepper flakes and dried oregano	Pinch

Citrus Dressing: In jar with tight-fitting lid, shake together orange juice, lemon juice, oil, green onion, garlic, salt, pepper, sugar, hot pepper flakes and oregano. Dressing can be refrigerated for up to 2 days; shake well to recombine.

In large salad bowl, toss together greens, mushrooms, onion and avocado. Pour on dressing and toss to coat. Serve immediately. Makes 8 servings.

You can refrigerate the zesty dressing until you toss it with this colorful salad. Use whatever lettuce looks crisp and good in the market — romaine, Boston, radicchio, endive. In terms of quantities, you'll probably need something like a head of romaine and one of Boston. Wash the greens ahead, dry them well and place in plastic bags with lots of paper towels to absorb any moisture.

APRICOT-RUM POUND CAKE

This slightly tart cake is easily transported, but better yet, it improves in flavor yet stays moist if it is made a few days in advance.

2/3 cup	chopped dried apricots (about 4 oz/125 g)	150 mL
1-3/4 cups	all-purpose flour	425 mL
1 cup	unsalted butter, at room temperature	250 mL
3/4 cup	granulated sugar	175 mL
4	eggs	4
2 tbsp	dark rum	25 mL
1 tsp	vanilla	5 mL
1 tsp	baking powder	5 mL
1/4 tsp	salt	1 mL
Rum Syrup:		
1/2 cup	granulated sugar	125 mL
1/4 cup	each water and dark rum	50 mL
Glaze:		
1/2 cup	icing sugar	125 mL
1 tbsp	(approx) whipping cream	15 mL
1/2 tsp	vanilla	2 mL

Lightly butter and flour 6-cup (1.5 L) tube pan. Dredge apricots with 1/4 cup (50 mL) of the flour and set aside.

In large bowl, cream butter thoroughly; gradually beat in sugar, beating until light and fluffy. Add eggs, one at a time, beating well after each addition. Stir in rum and vanilla.

Sift remaining 1-1/2 cups (375 mL) flour with baking powder and salt. Add to creamed mixture, stirring only until combined. Fold in floured apricots. Spoon into prepared pan. Bake in 325°F (160°C) oven for 55 to 60 minutes or until tester inserted in centre comes out clean. Cool in pan for 5 minutes; invert on wire rack set over waxed paper.

Rum Syrup: Meanwhile, in small saucepan, combine sugar and water; stir over medium heat until sugar is dissolved. Bring to full rolling boil; remove from heat and stir in rum.

With skewer, make several holes down through top of hot cake. Pour warm syrup over top. Let cool completely.

Glaze: Stir together icing sugar, cream and vanilla, adding more cream if necessary to make smooth thin glaze. Drizzle over cooled cake, letting it run down sides. Store in tightly covered container in cool place for several days or freeze for longer storage. Makes 8 servings.

Weekend Get-Together for Eight

Oven-Fried Almonds

Make-Ahead Paella

*Hearts of Palm and Avocado Salad
with Greens and Lime Vinaigrette*

Candied Lemon Tart

When people really enjoy cooking and entertaining, sometimes part of the pleasure comes with shopping in favorite markets and shops for those little extras you don't serve every day.

Plan this easy-to-serve menu on a weekend when you can go to your favorite fish market for the seafood, pick up chorizo at a Portuguese or Spanish grocery store, seek out really fresh whole almonds and discover a good-quality hearts of palm at your local deli.

If time evaporates while I'm preparing for this party, I cheat by buying a delicious lemon curd available at our local market. I spoon it into tiny baked tart shells, garnish each with a candied violet and present the tarts on a pretty plate, as shown on the front cover photo.

Everything can be prepared ahead so that you can relax with friends and enjoy the fruits of your shopping.

PARTY PRIMER

1. *Up to two weeks ahead, prepare Oven-Fried Almonds.*
2. *Up to two days ahead, wash and dry greens for salad.*
3. *Up to one day ahead, make Lime Vinaigrette. Put together paella.*
4. *Early in the day, prepare Candied Lemon Tart.*
5. *Up to two hours ahead, toss greens with hearts of palm and onion.*
6. *About one hour before serving, finish paella.*
7. *Toss greens with avocado and salad dressing.*

OVEN-FRIED ALMONDS

4 cups	whole blanched almonds	1 L
1 tbsp	olive oil	15 mL
1/2 tsp	(approx) coarse salt	2 mL

Scatter nuts on baking sheet; drizzle with oil and toss to coat. Roast in 400°F (200°C) oven for 10 to 15 minutes or until golden brown, tossing once or twice.

Sprinkle with salt, adding more to taste; toss and let cool. Spread out on paper towels to drain. (Almonds can be stored in covered container for up to 2 weeks.) Makes 4 cups (1 L).

This appetizer is simple and very quick to make, but irresistible with before-dinner drinks.

THE WINE

The whole feeling of this meal is relaxed, easy-going and very Spanish, so the wines you choose should be no-fuss, too.

The Spanish would have half a bottle of lightly chilled Fino or Manzanilla sherry with the Almonds, and the combination would be perfect. If you would prefer wine, choose a full-bodied white from a hot growing region such as the Rhône Valley (Côtes-du-Rhône white) or Sicily (Corvo, Regaleali).

MAKE-AHEAD PAELLA

16	large mussels (about 1 lb/500 g)	16
1/2 lb	fresh medium shrimp	250 g
3 lb	chicken thighs and drumsticks	1.5 kg
	Salt and pepper	
1/4 cup	olive oil	50 mL
1 lb	chorizo or other spicy smoked sausage	500 g
1	large onion, finely chopped	1
2	cloves garlic, minced	2
1	each sweet green and red pepper, cut in strips	1
2	tomatoes, peeled, seeded and chopped	2
2 cups	parboiled rice	500 mL
1/4 tsp	saffron, crushed	1 mL
4-1/2 cups	boiling water	1.125 L
2 cups	fresh or frozen (not thawed) green peas	500 mL
2 tbsp	chopped fresh parsley	25 mL
2	lemons, cut in wedges	2

Paella was originally made outdoors, cooked over an open fire and eaten by families as they worked in the fields of Spain. Now, this classic meal-in-one-dish is an easy way to entertain some special people indoors. Vary the seafood according to what you like and what is fresh in the market.

Scrub mussels, removing beards; discard any that do not close tightly. Refrigerate in bowl covered with damp tea towel. Shell and devein shrimp, leaving tails intact. Cover and refrigerate.

Dry chicken well; season with salt and pepper. In large skillet, heat half of the oil; brown chicken on all sides, in batches, transferring to paella pan or large shallow casserole as pieces brown.

Slice sausage thinly and add to skillet; brown for about 7 minutes. Remove to paella pan.

Drain off all fat in skillet. Heat remaining oil over medium-high heat; cook onion, garlic, pepper strips and tomatoes, stirring constantly, until thickened and most of the liquid evaporates. Remove from heat. Add rice and stir to coat. Stir in I tsp (5 mL) salt and saffron. Scrape contents of skillet into paella pan around chicken and sausage. (Recipe can be prepared to this point, covered and refrigerated for up to I day. Remove from refrigerator 30 minutes before proceeding.)

Stir in water and bring to boil; reduce heat to low and simmer, covered, for 20 minutes or until rice is almost tender. Add mussels, cover and steam for 5 minutes; discard any that do not open. Add shrimp and peas; cover and cook for 5 minutes or until shrimp are pink. Garnish with parsley and lemon wedges to serve. (Alternatively, cover and bake in 375°F/190°C oven for 25 minutes. Arrange mussels, shrimp and peas on top; bake, covered, for 15 minutes or until mussels open.) Makes 8 servings.

THE WINE

The wealth of taste sensations in the Paella make this a difficult dish to match with wine. The seafood flavors, the chicken, the spicy sausage and the sweet peppers combine with contradictory tastes. As a rule of thumb, always go with the wines of the region in which the dish originated – that calls for Spanish reds or rosés.

International option: Rioja red or rosé (Spain) or Oregon Pinot Noir or lightly chilled Beaujolais Crus (one of the named villages: Fleurie, Morgon, Regnié, etc.) or lightly chilled Valpolicella.

Canadian option: Ontario Gamay Beaujolais or Pinot Noir.

White wine option: Sauvignon Blanc from the Loire (Sancerre or Pouilly-Fumé) or California Sauvignon Blanc.

Hearts of Palm and Avocado Salad with Greens and Lime Vinaigrette

1	can (398 mL) hearts of palm	1
12 cups	torn mixed salad greens	3 L
1	small red onion, thinly sliced	1
1	large avocado, peeled and sliced	1

Lime Vinaigrette:

1/2 tsp	grated lime zest	2 mL
2 tbsp	fresh lime juice	25 mL
2 tsp	Dijon mustard	10 mL
Pinch	hot pepper flakes	Pinch
	Salt and pepper	
1/3 cup	olive oil	75 mL

Lime Vinaigrette: In small bowl, whisk together lime zest, lime juice, mustard, hot pepper flakes, and salt and pepper to taste; gradually whisk in oil. (Vinaigrette can be covered and refrigerated for up to 1 day. Whisk just before using.)

Rinse hearts of palm and dry well; cut into bite-sized pieces to make about 2 cups (500 mL). In salad bowl, toss together hearts of palm, greens and onion. (Salad can be loosely covered with damp towel and refrigerated for up to 4 hours.) Just before serving, add avocado. Toss with vinaigrette. Makes 8 servings.

Hearts of palm have a refreshingly tart flavor, and with the lime dressing, this salad makes a delicious foil for the main course.

Candied Lemon Tart

2	large lemons	2
	Pastry for 9-inch (23 cm) single-crust pie	
1/4 cup	unsalted butter	50 mL
1-1/3 cups	granulated sugar	325 mL
1	egg	1
1 tbsp	finely grated lemon zest	15 mL
1/4 tsp	almond extract	1 mL
1/2 cup	ground blanched almonds	125 mL
1 tbsp	all-purpose flour	15 mL
1/4 tsp	vanilla	1 mL

With sharp knife, slice lemons as thinly as possible, still keeping slices whole. Place in heatproof bowl and cover with boiling water; let stand, covered, for 6 hours.

Drain slices and place in saucepan; cover with fresh cold water and bring to boil. Drain again and cover with fresh cold water; bring

This is the simple, elegant tart you see in smart pastry shop windows. Although there are various steps, they can be done in stages for a completely make-ahead company dessert. Add a tablespoon (15 mL) of sugar to your favorite regular pastry recipe or use a sweet short-crust pastry (see page 130).

to boil. Reduce heat, cover and simmer for 30 minutes or until rinds are soft and pulp has partly disintegrated. Let cool in liquid.

On lightly floured surface, roll out pastry and line tart tin (preferably with removable bottom). Prick bottom all over with fork and line with parchment paper or foil. Fill with dried beans or rice and bake in 400°F (200°C) oven for 5 minutes. Remove paper and beans; set aside.

In bowl, beat butter with 1/3 cup (75 mL) of the sugar until light and fluffy. Beat egg lightly; stir in lemon zest and almond extract. Gradually blend into butter mixture. Stir together almonds and flour; blend into butter mixture. Spread evenly over partially baked pastry; bake in 375°F (190°) oven for 25 to 30 minutes or until puffed, golden brown and firm to the touch. Cool.

Meanwhile, reserving 1 cup (250 mL) of th liquid, drain lemon slices in sieve. In saucepan, combine reserved liquid, remaining 1 cup (250 mL) sugar and vanilla; cook over low heat until sugar is dissolved. Add lemon slices and simmer, uncovered, for 5 minutes. Transfer lemon slices to plate and boil syrup until small amount on cold saucer crinkles when pushed with finger, 18 to 20 minutes. Arrange lemon slices attractively (overlapping somewhat) over tart; spoon hot syrup on top. Let cool to room temperature to serve. Makes 8 servings.

THE WINE

The acidity of the lemon flavor calls for a dessert wine with equal acidity. This suggests Ontario Icewine or German Eiswein. Icewine is expensive. You could substitute a Late Harvest Riesling from Ontario or B.C., or an Austrian Beerenauslese.

A Simple Curry Supper for Four or Six

Poppadums

Beef Curry

Cooked White Rice

Raisin Chutney

Yogurt with Cucumber and Tomato

Mango Sorbet with Fresh Fruit

I'm leaving it up to you to know the appetites of your guests as to whether this simple meal will satisfy four or six people. My family love it so much that it will nicely do the four of us. Of course, any left-over curry is excellent reheated or frozen for another time.

Thin, crisp and delicious discs, poppadums are readily available at shops that sell East Indian ingredients. You can buy spicy or plain poppadums and count on about two and a half per person. You can heat them in the microwave, two or three at a time wrapped in paper towels; or, fry two at a time (so they won't curl up) in hot oil, turning them once; or, broil about 3 inches (8 cm) from the element.

PARTY PRIMER

1. *Up to two weeks ahead, make Raisin Chutney.*
2. *Up to two days ahead, make Beef Curry.*
3. *At least eight hours ahead, make Mango Sorbet.*
4. *Cook White Rice. Reheat curry and sprinkle with coriander.*
5. *Just before serving, heat poppadums. Prepare Yogurt with Cucumber and Tomato.*

Beef Curry

1-1/2 lb	lean beef (round steak or chuck)	750 g
3	cloves garlic, crushed	3
2 tbsp	minced fresh ginger	25 mL
1-1/2 tsp	each ground turmeric (approx), ground cumin and ground coriander	7 mL
1 tsp	salt	5 mL
Pinch	hot pepper flakes	Pinch
2 tbsp	(approx) vegetable oil	25 mL
4	onions, chopped	4
1 tsp	each ground cloves and cinnamon	5 mL
1	can (19 oz/540 mL) tomatoes	1
	Chopped fresh coriander	

Cut beef into 1-inch (2.5 cm) cubes. In small heatproof bowl, combine beef, garlic, ginger, turmeric, cumin, coriander, salt and hot pepper flakes, mixing well with hands. Cover with foil and let stand at room temperature for 30 minutes.

In large saucepan, heat oil over medium heat; cook onions for 7 minutes, stirring often. Stir in cloves, cinnamon and pinch more turmeric; push to one side of pan.

With slotted spoon, transfer meat to pan; cook, stirring often and adding more oil if necessary, until meat loses its pinkness. Stir in meat juices that have accumulated in bowl along with tomatoes; bring to boil. Reduce heat to low; cover and simmer for about 1-1/2 hours or until meat is very tender, stirring occasionally. (Curry can be cooled, covered and refrigerated for up to 2 days. Reheat slowly, stirring often.) Taste and adjust seasoning if necessary. Sprinkle with coriander to serve. Makes 4 to 6 servings.

Note: If you have a pressure cooker, put a little water in it and place foil-covered bowl of beef cubes on rack inside. Pressure-cook for 10 minutes to draw out juices. If you have no cooker, omit this step.

When I lived in London, Ontario, our next-door neighbor taught me to make this very delicious curry with spices her father sent to her from Bombay. It's a simple recipe that I've made ever since for our own family or for friends who love the fascinating mix of East Indian flavors. It's a good dish for company because it's even better to make one day and serve the next and it is quite inexpensive. If you like curries hotter, add more crushed chilies.

I set out little dishes of raisins and peanuts so that guests can add a sprinkle of each if they want.

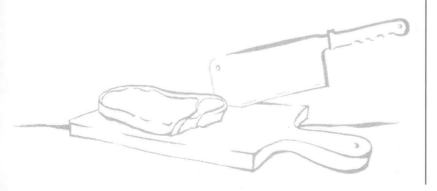

THE WINE

Normally I would not suggest a wine with curry. The spices — coriander, cumin, turmeric, cloves and cinnamon — overpower virtually anything you put beside them. But Rose has given me a challenge here. If you are bound and determined to have wine, you can go with either a sweetish, full-bodied red such as a Recioto della Valpolicella from Veneto, or a spicy white such as a Gewürztraminer from Alsace. Otherwise, have a beer.

COOKED WHITE RICE

Rice is a perfect accompaniment to Beef Curry, especially if the rice you choose is Basmati. If rice is not a regular item on the menu at your house, this is the method of cooking with measured water. If using parboiled rice, use 1/2 cup (125 mL) more water and cook about 5 minutes longer.

1-1/2 cups	long-grain rice	375 mL
3 cups	water	750 mL
1 tsp	salt	5 mL
4 tsp	butter	20 mL

If using basmati rice, spread in single layer on large tray; pick out any foreign matter, rinse well and drain. (This is not necessary for regular long-grain or parboiled rice.)

In large pot, bring water to boil. Add salt and stir; add rice and stir in butter. Cover and reduce heat to low; cook for 15 to 20 minutes or until grains are tender and water has been absorbed. Let stand for 5 minutes; fluff with fork and serve. Makes 6 servings.

RAISIN CHUTNEY

In the teaching days at my cooking school, one of my students shared this simple chutney with our class the night we did an East Indian menu. It takes only minutes to make, is composed of ordinary ingredients and keeps in the refrigerator for about two weeks. I love it with Beef Curry.

1 cup	raisins	250 mL
1 tbsp	chopped fresh ginger	15 mL
1/2 tsp	each salt and cayenne pepper	2 mL
1/4 cup	cold water	50 mL
4 tsp	fresh lemon juice	20 mL

Put raisins, ginger, salt, cayenne, water and lemon juice in blender. Blend to form coarse paste. (Chutney can be refrigerated in airtight container for up to 2 weeks.) Makes about 1 cup (250 mL).

YOGURT WITH CUCUMBER AND TOMATO

1 cup	plain low-fat yogurt	250 mL
1	English cucumber (unpeeled), diced	1
1/4 cup	minced white onion	50 mL
2 tbsp	chopped fresh coriander	25 mL
1/2 tsp	ground cumin	2 mL
Pinch	cayenne pepper	Pinch
	Salt and pepper	
1	firm ripe tomato, diced	1

In bowl, stir together yogurt, cucumber, onion, coriander, cumin, cayenne, and salt and pepper to taste. Gently stir in tomato. Serve immediately. Makes 4 to 6 servings.

I love an excuse to make a raita like this since I could sit down to a bowl of it with any kind of meal — even a barbecued steak. I like to dice the vegetables coarsely so that it's more like a salad.

MANGO SORBET

1 cup	water	250 mL
1/2 cup	granulated sugar	125 mL
2 cups	cubed peeled ripe mangoes	500 mL
3/4 cup	fresh orange juice	175 mL
1/4 cup	fresh lime juice	50 mL

In saucepan, bring water and sugar to boil over high heat; boil rapidly, uncovered, for about 5 minutes or until reduced to 2/3 cup (150 mL). Let cool and chill.

In food processor or blender, purée mangoes, orange juice, lime juice and chilled syrup. Transfer to ice-cream maker and freeze according to manufacturer's directions.

(Or, pour into shallow cake pan; freeze until firm, about 4 hours. Purée in food processor until smooth and creamy; pack into airtight container and refreeze for 4 hours or until firm.) Makes 4 to 6 servings.

Let the sorbet stand for a few minutes at room temperature to soften slightly before serving. Arrange a few extra slices of fresh mango or other fruit on the side of each serving.

THE WINE

The curry flavors linger on the palate. The idea of the mango sorbet and fresh fruit is to cleanse and refresh the palate, so don't gild the lily with a dessert wine. Once you have finished, try an eau-de-vie (Framboise or Pear William).

PRINCIPLES FOR SERVING WINE THROUGHOUT A MEAL

1. Dry wines before sweeter ones.   Beginning a meal with a sweet wine tends to dull the palate while a dry white wine (still or sparkling) stimulates appetite. A dry wine taken after a sweeter one will accentuate the acidity and make it taste sharp.

2. Chilled wines before room-temperature wines.   A wine that has spent time in the ice bucket or refrigerator will anesthetize the palate to some extent. All whites are chilled, which means whites before reds (unless you are having a sweet dessert wine as the last wine of the meal).

3. White wines before red wines.   Red wines generally have more body and more complexity than whites. If you taste a white after a red, it will seem thin and highly acidic. Again, the exception is sweet white dessert wine.

4. Younger wines before older wines.   Older wines exhibit more bouquet and complex flavors than younger wines. Work up to the best wine of the evening. If you serve your best wine first, all of the others will suffer by comparison.

5. Light-bodied wines before full-bodied wines.   Drinking a Beaujolais after a Côtes-du-Rhône or a Mosel Riesling after an Australian Chardonnay is rather like having your consommé after the pheasant *pâté en croute*. The residual taste of the one wine will overpower the delicacy of the other.

6. Match the weight of the wine with the weight of the food.   This doesn't mean putting them each on the scales. A heavy wine will overpower a delicate dish. Avoid heavy, oaky whites with delicate fish, and light, fruity reds with highly spiced meat stews and casseroles.

7. Light wines at lunch, fuller-bodied wines at dinner.   Don't serve powerful reds and luscious dessert wines at lunch. They're too heavy to enjoy unless you want to sleep them off. Save them for dinner. Choose lighter wines in keeping with the lunchtime menu, particularly whites and rosés.

8. Wines of the same region.   If you're serving a range of wines, try to select them from the same region. This way your guests can compare vintages or estates. Red Burgundy and Bordeaux don't work well together, but if you want that combination, drink the Bordeaux first.

9. Avoid winter wines in summer.   Winter wines are those that are best consumed when the weather is cold – hearty, powerful red wines (such as Châteauneuf-du-Pâpe and Zinfandel). The heat of summer demands light, refreshing wines that you can chill – including the reds.

10. Avoid imbalanced marriages.   Don't serve a great wine (such as a well-aged Château-bottled claret) with a hot dog. By the same token, don't open the $6 a litre special with caviar.

11. Select your wines to balance one another.   Plan your menu to ensure that the dishes complement one another, that you don't have too many rich sauces or a delicately flavored dish following a highly spiced one. Think of your wines in the same way.

12. A fine wine deserves a fine glass.   Wine tastes better out of a good glass, one that is thin, without any color (so you can see the wine), with a decent stem and a shape that concentrates the bouquet in the glass – that is, the radius of its belly is larger than its aperture.

Friday Night Designer Pizza Party

Grilled Eggplant and Goat Cheese Pizza

Pizza with Sun-Dried Tomatoes and Broccoli

Roasted Red Pepper Pizza with Prosciutto

Smoked Salmon and Dill Pizza

Mocha-Almond Crunch Torte

I must admit, visiting someone who insists on leaving the television on is not much of a visit. We have good friends, however, who love classic movies and very occasionally, we invite them over for a *Casablanca* night or even an evening of the world's worst movies. Have you ever seen *Attack of the Killer Tomatoes?*

For such an event, a formal sit-down dinner is just not appropriate. Pizza is perfect — especially homemade pizzas. They are so delicious and not really difficult to make. The dough recipe is a cinch, but you can always cheat and buy some from the local pizza parlor.

This is a pretty flexible menu; all four pizzas will serve eight, but make the number you need for the number of guests your have. It's also a great chance to have a co-op effort; everyone can pitch in to slice, chop and grate.

All the pizzas are baked at a fairly high temperature. A bit of cornmeal sprinkled onto the pan before pressing the dough onto it will keep the bottom of the crust from getting too brown, if your oven has that tendency. In any event, watch them closely as they bake.

PARTY PRIMER

1. *Up to two months or up to eight hours ahead, make and freeze or refrigerate Pizza Dough if making ahead. Otherwise, prepare up to three hours ahead.*
2. *Up to three days ahead, make and freeze Mocha-Almond Crunch Torte.*
3. *Up to one day or one hour ahead, roast and marinate peppers for Red Pepper Pizza and refrigerate or leave at room temperature.*
4. *Up to two hours ahead, grill eggplant for Goat Cheese Pizza.*
5. *Just before mealtime, garnish and refrigerate torte.*
6. *Finish pizza toppings and bake.*

Grilled Eggplant and Goat Cheese Pizza

5	tiny Italian eggplants	5
1/4 cup	olive oil	50 mL
	Pizza Dough for 12-inch (30 cm) pizza (recipe page 74)	
1/4 tsp	hot pepper flakes	1 mL
2 cups	shredded mozzarella cheese	500 mL
3/4 cup	tomato sauce	175 mL
1 cup	diced or crumbled goat cheese (1/4 lb/125 g)	250 mL
1/2 tsp	dried basil	2 mL

The mild cheeses in this pizza make it a good choice for the more conservative fan.

Trim and thinly slice eggplants lengthwise; brush with some of the oil. Grill, broil or sauté until well browned on both sides, being careful not to burn. Drain on paper towels. (Eggplant can be set aside for up to 2 hours.)

Press dough onto greased pizza pan. Brush lightly with some of the oil; sprinkle with hot pepper flakes and half of the mozzarella. Spread with tomato sauce; arrange eggplant slices on top. Sprinkle with remaining mozzarella, goat cheese and basil; drizzle with remaining oil. Bake in 500° F (260°C) oven for 12 to 15 minutes or until crust is golden brown. Makes 2 or 3 servings.

Pizza with Sun-Dried Tomatoes and Broccoli

1 tbsp	(approx) olive oil	15 mL
1	clove garlic, minced	1
2 cups	sliced mushrooms	500 mL
1/2 cup	sun-dried tomatoes (oil-packed)	125 mL
1/2 cup	chopped black olives	125 mL
1/2 tsp	each dried oregano and basil	2 mL
	Pizza Dough for 12-inch (30 cm) pizza (recipe page 74)	
2 cups	shredded provolone cheese	500 mL
1-1/2 cups	small broccoli florets	375 mL
1 tbsp	oil from sun-dried tomatoes (or more olive oil)	15 mL

Provolone is a mellow Italian cheese that shouldn't be overlooked when making pizzas. Here it makes a good background flavor for intense sun-dried tomatoes and fresh broccoli.

In skillet, heat 1 tbsp (15 mL) oil over medium heat; cook garlic and mushrooms for 3 minutes. Remove from heat. Cut tomatoes into thin strips; stir into mushrooms. Add olives, oregano and basil.

Press dough onto greased pizza pan; brush lightly with oil. Sprinkle with two-thirds of the cheese; top with mushroom mixture. Scatter broccoli over top; sprinkle with remaining cheese and drizzle with tomato oil. Bake in 475°F (240°C) oven for 12 to 15 minutes or until crust is golden brown. Makes 2 or 3 servings.

ROASTED RED PEPPER PIZZA WITH PROSCIUTTO

Smoky roasted peppers, piquant prosciutto and nutty fontina cheese give this pizza lots of pleasant flavors.

2	sweet red peppers	2
1 tbsp	finely chopped fresh parsley	15 mL
2	cloves garlic, minced	2
1/2 tsp	dried thyme	2 mL
	Salt and pepper	
	Olive oil	
	Pizza Dough for 12-inch (30 cm) pizza (recipe page 74)	
3 cups	shredded fontina cheese	750 mL
4 oz	thinly sliced prosciutto	125 g

Roast peppers under broiler, on grill, or in 450°F (230°C) oven for about 15 minutes or until charred and blistered, turning often. Remove and place under overturned bowl to steam for 10 minutes. Peel, seed and cut into thin strips.

In bowl, combine peppers, parsley, garlic, thyme, and salt and pepper to taste; drizzle with 1 tbsp (15 mL) olive oil. Let marinate at room temperature for 1 hour or up to 24 hours in refrigerator.

Press dough onto greased pizza pan. Brush lightly with oil; sprinkle with two-thirds of the cheese. Cut prosciutto into thin strips and scatter on top. Arrange red pepper mixture over top, using spatula to scrape bowl clean. Sprinkle with more pepper to taste and remaining cheese; drizzle with about 1 tbsp (15 mL) oil. Bake in 500°F (260°C) oven for 12 to 15 minutes or until crust is golden brown. Makes 2 or 3 servings.

Smoked Salmon and Dill Pizza

	Pizza Dough for 12-inch (30 cm) pizza (recipe follows)	
	Vegetable oil	
1	large tomato, seeded and diced	1
1/2 cup	sliced green onions	125 mL
1	large clove garlic, minced	1
1 tbsp	snipped fresh dill	15 mL
1/4 tsp	pepper	1 mL
6 oz	fontina or Asiago cheese, grated	175 g
1/4 lb	smoked salmon, cut in 2-inch (5 cm) julienne strips	125 g
1 tbsp	capers	15 mL

Press dough onto greased pizza pan; brush with 1-1/2 tsp (7 mL) oil.

In small bowl, gently stir together tomato, onions, garlic, dill and pepper; scatter over dough, leaving 3/4-inch (2 cm) border. Sprinkle with cheese; drizzle with 1 tbsp (15 mL) oil. Bake in 475°F (240°C) oven for 12 minutes.

Remove from oven and arrange salmon and capers on top; drizzle with 1 tbsp (15 mL) oil. Bake for 3 to 5 minutes longer or until crust is golden brown. Makes 2 or 3 servings.

If you wish to be extravagant, add a bit of black caviar to this fun pizza.

Pizza Dough

Pinch	granulated sugar	Pinch
2/3 cup	warm water	150 mL
2 tsp	active dry yeast	10 mL
2 tbsp	vegetable oil	25 mL
1-1/2 cups	(approx) all-purpose flour	375 mL
1/2 tsp	salt	2 mL

In small bowl, combine sugar and water; sprinkle yeast over top and let stand in warm place until bubbly and doubled in volume, about 5 minutes. Stir in oil.

In large bowl, mix flour with salt; make well in centre and pour in yeast mixture. With fork, gradually blend together to form dough. With floured hands, gather into ball.

Turn out onto lightly floured surface; knead for about 5 minutes, adding just enough extra flour to make soft, slightly sticky dough. Place in greased bowl, turning once to grease all over. Cover

You can double or triple this recipe to have ready and waiting for your pizza party. The dough can be rolled out, wrapped and refrigerated on a pan for up to 8 hours or frozen. Or wrap the risen dough in plastic wrap, then in plastic bag before freezing. Thaw before rolling out.

with greased waxed paper and tea towel. Let stand in warm draft-free place until tripled in volume, 1-1/2 to 3 hours.

Punch down dough and form into ball. Turn out onto lightly floured surface and cover with bowl; let stand for 10 minutes. Roll out dough into 12-inch (30 cm) circle. Makes one 12-inch (30 cm) crust.

THE WINE

Instead of your elegant, long-stemmed wine glasses, why not go totally Italian bistro and use the kitchen tumblers? Since you'll probably be eating this off your knees or sitting on the floor watching old movies, you'll want a wine that doesn't demand much attention. My preference would be an Italian white with good acidity to combat the smoked salmon and dill flavors if you are going to serve all four pizzas together.

International option: Pinot Grigio (Northern Italy), Sancerre (Loire), Rioja white (Spain), New Zealand Sauvignon Blanc.

Canadian option: B.C. Pinot Blanc, Ontario Auxerrois or Aligoté.

If you want to put on the dog and supply a wine for each of the pizza flavors, here goes:

Eggplant and Goat Cheese: Sauvignon Blanc (Loire, New Zealand or Sonoma Valley).

Sun-Dried Tomatoes and Broccoli: Chilled Bardolino or Barbera (Italy).

Roasted Red Pepper with Prosciutto: Alsatian Sylvaner or Pinot Blanc, Italian Chardonnay.

Smoked Salmon with Dill: Mosel Riesling Trocken, Alsatian Gewürztraminer.

MOCHA-ALMOND CRUNCH TORTE

1/2 cup	ground almonds	125 mL
8 oz	semisweet chocolate	250 g
1 cup	whipping cream	250 mL
1/4 cup	unsalted butter	50 mL
2 tbsp	corn syrup	25 mL
4 cups	mocha ice cream, softened	1 L
1 cup	toasted sliced almonds	250 mL
1 tbsp	amaretto	15 mL
Garnish:		
1 cup	whipping cream	250 mL
4 tsp	instant coffee granules	20 mL
1/2 cup	icing sugar	125 mL
1/2 cup	toasted sliced almonds	125 mL
12	chocolate-coated coffee beans	12

This easy dessert is filled with the flavors of chocolate fudge, mocha ice cream and toasted almonds. It can be made ahead and frozen for up to three days. Transfer to the refrigerator 30 minutes before serving to soften slightly.

Butter 8-inch (2 L) springform pan; sprinkle bottom and sides with ground almonds, shaking pan to coat bottom evenly. Set aside.

In double boiler over simmering water, melt chocolate with cream. Remove from heat and stir in butter until melted; stir in corn syrup. Transfer to bowl; place over ice in larger bowl. Stir until just thickened, about 5 minutes. Pour into prepared pan; cover and refrigerate for at least 1 hour or chill in freezer until firm.

In chilled bowl, combine ice cream, sliced almonds and amaretto. Spoon over chilled chocolate layer; cover and freeze for at least 4 hours or until ice-cream layer is firm.

Garnish: In small saucepan, heat 1/4 cup (50 mL) of the cream and coffee granules over low heat until coffee dissolves. Transfer to large bowl; refrigerate until cold. Beat in remaining cream and icing sugar until stiff.

Run knife around edge of torte. Remove sides and bottom of pan; transfer torte to serving plate. Garnish sides with almonds. Pipe coffee-flavored whipped cream decoratively on top, reserving most of the cream for rosettes. Pipe 12 rosettes around top; place chocolate-coated coffee bean in centre of each. Makes 8 to 12 servings.

THE WINE

There is really no wine that can stand up to this Torte's calorie attack except perhaps Cream Sherry or Amaretto. Best have nothing at all and finish off the evening with a grappa.

FOOD PREPARATION HINT

Poaching eggs:

Eggs have to be perfectly fresh to poach properly. A fresh egg will form a neat oval with the white all around the yolk. Older eggs are apt to produce wispy whites and exposed yolks. To test for freshness, place an egg in a glass of water. If it lies on its side, it's fresh. If it sits upright, switch your menu to scrambled eggs.

To poach eggs, fill wide shallow saucepan or large deep skillet with about 2 inches (5 cm) water and add 2 tbsp (25 mL) white vinegar; bring to simmer. Cooking only four eggs in each batch (or using two pans), crack each egg, hold very close to water, open shell and gently slip egg in. Rapidly roll egg over and over with wooden spoon so that white is turned over yolk in a neat oval. Poach in barely simmering water for 2 to 3 minutes or until yolks are of desired consistency. Test by gently touching egg with finger. Yolk should be soft and fairly set; white should be just set.

To poach eggs ahead, undercook slightly. Yolk should feel wobbly. With slotted spoon, remove eggs immediately and submerge in bowl of ice water; refrigerate, uncovered, for up to three days. If the whites are wispy, you can trim them with scissors before submerging in the ice water. To reheat, use a slotted spoon and drop eggs into barely simmering water to heat for about 2 minutes.

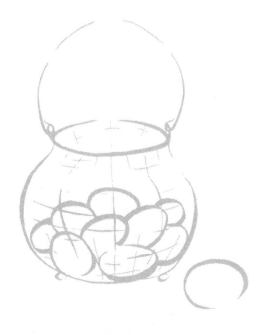

Welcome Spring Brunch for Eight

Raspberry Champagne

Fresh Fruit Salad with Orange Cream

Spicy Oatmeal Muffins

Cinnamon Twists

Eggs Benedict with Salmon

Steamed Asparagus

Mixed Greens and Herbs with Honey Vinaigrette

Rhubarb Custard Torte

*I*n this country where winter outlasts its welcome, I always like to greet Spring with special celebration. One of my favorite ways of doing this is to invite good friends for brunch and while away a warm, sunny Sunday with relaxing talk and food.

I greet each guest with Raspberry Champagne, which I make by splashing each chilled flute glass with enough raspberry-flavored brandy or raspberry liqueur to tint champagne a light pink before filling with champagne. I offer fruit and muffins as soon as people arrive, then I take my time getting into the main course after everyone has come.

Although there are a few quick last-minute details like making toast and warming the eggs, most things can be completely prepared the day before.

PARTY PRIMER

1. *Up to three days ahead, poach eggs for Eggs Benedict and refrigerate in water.*
2. *Up to two days ahead, prepare greens for salad.*
3. *One day ahead, make Honey Vinaigrette. Marinate fruit for Fruit Salad. Prepare Cinnamon Twists for baking and refrigerate; make glaze. Make Rhubarb Custard Torte.*
4. *Early in the morning, make and bake Spicy Oatmeal Muffins. Bake and glaze Twists.*
5. *Up to one hour ahead, make Yogurt Hollandaise and leave at room temperature. Tear and toss greens for salad.*
6. *Just before serving, make Orange Cream for fruit.*
7. *Just before mealtime, garnish torte.*
8. *Just before serving, toast bread, reheat eggs and assemble Eggs Benedict. Toss salad with dressing.*

THE WINE

To economize, choose a dry sparkling wine from Spain or Sekt from Germany to make the Raspberry Champagne.

FRESH FRUIT SALAD WITH ORANGE CREAM

2 cups	seedless green grapes	500 mL
2 cups	orange segments (about 4 oranges)	500 mL
2 cups	sliced peeled kiwifruit	500 mL
2 cups	sliced strawberries	500 mL
1/4 cup	fresh orange juice	50 mL
1/4 cup	Grand Marnier, other orange	50 mL
	liqueur or additional orange juice	
2/3 cup	whipping cream	150 mL
2 tsp	each icing sugar and grated orange zest	10 mL
2 tbsp	sour cream	25 mL

In 8-cup (2 L) measuring cup or narrow bowl, layer fruit with grapes on bottom, then oranges, kiwifruit and strawberries. Pour in orange juice and Grand Marnier. Do not stir. Cover and refrigerate for at least 1 hour or up to 24 hours.

Just before serving, whip cream with icing sugar and orange zest for 1 minute. Add sour cream and beat for 3 minutes.

Stir fruit and transfer to pretty glass bowl. Serve with orange cream in small serving bowl. Makes 8 servings.

A wee dollop of orange-flavored cream and a bit of liqueur turn a simple but colorful fruit salad into company fare. If you wish, use crème fraîche instead of whipping and sour cream. Serve the fruit at room temperature for best flavor.

CINNAMON TWISTS

Pinch	granulated sugar	Pinch
1/4 cup	lukewarm water	50 mL
1	pkg active dry yeast (or 1 tbsp/15 mL)	1
3/4 cup	lukewarm sour cream	175 mL
Pinch	baking soda	Pinch
1/4 cup	granulated sugar	50 mL
1	egg	1
2 tbsp	soft shortening or lard	25 mL
3/4 tsp	salt	4 mL
2-1/2 cups	(approx) all-purpose flour	625 mL
2 tbsp	butter, softened	25 mL
1/3 cup	lightly packed brown sugar	75 mL
1 tsp	cinnamon	5 mL

These pretty little twists are easy to make and bake the morning of your brunch. Or make them the night before and just pop them into the oven for a few minutes before serving. Either way, guests will enjoy their fresh taste and aroma.

»

Glaze:

1/2 cup	icing sugar	125 mL
2 tbsp	butter, softened	25 mL
1 tsp	finely grated orange zest	5 mL
1 tbsp	fresh orange juice	15 mL

In measuring cup, dissolve pinch of sugar in lukewarm water. Sprinkle yeast over water and let stand for 10 minutes or until bubbly.

Meanwhile, in large warm bowl, stir together sour cream and soda. Stir in 1/4 cup (50 mL) granulated sugar, egg, shortening and salt. Stir yeast briskly with fork; blend into sour cream mixture. Stir in enough flour to make dough that is easy to handle and not too sticky.

Turn dough out onto floured surface; knead for about 5 minutes or until smooth and elastic, adding only enough flour to keep dough from sticking as you knead.

Using rolling pin, roll dough into 24- x 6-inch (60 x 15 cm) rectangle; spread with butter. Stir together brown sugar and cinnamon; sprinkle lengthwise over half of dough. Fold uncovered half over sugar mixture so edges meet; cut into 24 strips, each 1 inch (2.5 cm) wide and 3 inches (8 cm) long. Pinch ends to seal; twist ends in opposite directions about 4 turns to form twist. Place about 1 inch (2.5 cm) apart on 2 greased baking sheets.

Cover twists with greased waxed paper and clean tea towel. If baking right away, let rise in warm spot (on heating pad turned to low if possible) for about 1 hour or until almost doubled in bulk. If baking the next day, refrigerate and let come to room temperature before baking. Bake twists in 375°F (190°C) oven for 12 to 15 minutes or until golden. Don't overbake or bottoms will darken. Using spatula, remove to rack set on waxed paper.

Glaze: Meanwhile, in small bowl, cream together icing sugar, butter and orange zest. Gradually beat in orange juice until smooth. Spread over warm twists. Makes 2 dozen.

SPICY OATMEAL MUFFINS

1 cup	quick-cooking rolled oats	250 mL
1 cup	buttermilk or soured milk*	250 mL
1-1/3 cups	all-purpose flour	325 mL
1/2 cup	packed brown sugar	125 mL
1-1/2 tsp	baking powder	7 mL
1 tsp	baking soda	5 mL
1 tsp	ground cinnamon	5 mL
1/2 tsp	ground nutmeg	2 mL
1/2 tsp	salt	2 mL
2	eggs	2
1/4 cup	butter, melted and cooled	50 mL
1 cup	raisins	250 mL

In large bowl, combine oats and buttermilk; set aside. Sift or stir together flour, brown sugar, baking powder, baking soda, cinnamon, nutmeg and salt.

In small bowl, beat eggs and stir in butter; stir into oat mixture. Add flour mixture all at once; stir only until moistened. Fold in raisins. Do not overmix.

Fill greased muffin cups two-thirds full; bake in 400°F (200°C) oven for about 20 minutes or until tops are firm to the touch. Cool 5 minutes before serving. Makes one dozen.

*To sour milk, stir 1 tbsp (15 mL) vinegar or lemon juice into 1 cup (250 mL) milk and let stand for 15 minutes.

Serve these moist easily made muffins with the Fresh Fruit Salad with Orange Cream as people arrive with their morning appetites.

EGGS BENEDICT WITH SALMON

8	slices rye or pumpernickel bread, toasted and buttered	8
8	very thin slices smoked salmon	8
8	poached eggs (see Page 77)	8
	Yogurt Hollandaise (recipe follows)	
	Sprigs of parsley or watercress	
	Capers	

Place hot slices of toast on warm plates. Top each with slice of smoked salmon, then hot poached egg. Drizzle with Yogurt Hollandaise. Garnish with parsley and capers. Makes 8 servings.

Traditionally, Eggs Benedict are made with English muffin halves topped with ham, poached eggs and hollandaise sauce, but here, I've combined smoked salmon and toasted rye bread. Have the plates warming and broil the bread while you finish off the eggs so that everyone gets this course hot.

YOGURT HOLLANDAISE

Hollandaise sauce goes well with the asparagus and salmon as well as the eggs. Invite guests to dip the asparagus spears into the poached eggs as a special treat.

3/4 cup	plain low-fat yogurt	175 mL
2 tsp	fresh lemon juice	10 mL
3	egg yolks	3
1/2 tsp	Dijon mustard	2 mL
1/4 tsp	salt	1 mL
Pinch	white pepper	Pinch
Dash	hot pepper sauce	Dash

In top of double boiler, whisk together yogurt, lemon juice, egg yolks, mustard, salt, pepper and hot pepper sauce. Cook over simmering water, stirring constantly, for 8 to 12 minutes or until sauce is thickened and coats back of wooden spoon. (Sauce can be kept at room temperature for up to 1 hour; reheat gently in double boiler.) Taste and adjust seasoning. Makes about 1 cup (250 mL).

THE WINE

You'll be surprised how influential the taste of asparagus is, even with the strong smokiness of the salmon in the Eggs Benedict. So consider this when you choose your wine. Sauvignon Blanc is one grape that can have green vegetable overtones.

International option: Sancerre (Loire), New Zealand Sauvignon Blanc, California Fumé or white Bordeaux.

Canadian option: Seyval Blanc, dry Vidal, Aligoté.

MIXED GREENS AND HERBS WITH HONEY VINAIGRETTE

1	bunch watercress	1
1	bunch leaf lettuce or Boston lettuce, separated	1
1	head Belgian endive	1
Half	head radicchio	Half
1/2 cup	coarsely chopped fresh parsley	125 mL
2 tbsp	snipped chives	25 mL

Honey Vinaigrette:

1/2 cup	vegetable oil	125 mL
2 tbsp	white wine vinegar	25 mL
2 tbsp	fresh lemon juice	25 mL
1 tsp	liquid honey	5 mL
1/4 tsp	each Dijon mustard, salt and pepper	1 mL

Remove thick stems from watercress. Wash and dry watercress and lettuce well. Wrap loosely in paper towels and place in plastic bag in refrigerator for up to 2 days.

Honey Vinaigrette: In small glass jar with tight-fitting lid, shake together oil, vinegar, lemon juice, honey, mustard, salt and pepper. Refrigerate until just before using; shake jar well to recombine.

To assemble salad, wipe endive clean; core and separate leaves. Rinse radicchio; dry and separate into leaves. Tear watercress and lettuce into large bite-size pieces.

In large salad bowl and using hands, lightly toss together endive, radicchio, watercress and lettuce. Sprinkle with parsley and chives. (Salad may be prepared to this point, covered with tea towel and refrigerated for up to 1 hour.)

Just before serving, pour dressing over salad and toss well. Makes 8 servings.

Watercress heralds spring and it's teamed here with other greens and radicchio to provide an array of shades, flavors and textures. For another exciting hint of spring, substitute a scattering of fresh edible flowers — rose petals, pansies, day lilies, violets or chive blossoms for the radicchio. (Do not use any flowers that have been chemically sprayed.)

RHUBARB CUSTARD TORTE

3/4 cup	butter	175 mL
1/3 cup	granulated sugar	75 mL
2	egg yolks	2
2 cups	all-purpose flour	500 mL
1 tsp	baking powder	5 mL
1/2 tsp	salt	2 mL

Filling:

6 cups	chopped rhubarb, cut in 1-inch (2.5 cm) pieces (about 1-1/2 lb/750 g)	1.5 L
1/2 cup	granulated sugar	125 mL
1/4 cup	quick-cooking tapioca*	50 mL

This elegant torte with its tender shortbread crust will become a favorite way of enjoying the season's first fruit. If you use frozen rhubarb, place in large sieve and pour hot water over it for a few seconds before proceeding.

1/2 tsp	ground cinnamon	2 mL
1/4 cup	water	50 mL
6	eggs	6
2 cups	sour cream	500 mL
1/2 cup	packed brown sugar	125 mL
2 tsp	finely grated lemon zest	10 mL
1 tsp	vanilla	5 mL
Garnish:		
	Icing sugar	
	Grated lemon zest	

In large bowl and using electric mixer, cream together butter and sugar; add egg yolks and beat until light and fluffy. Sift or stir together flour, baking powder and salt; add to egg mixture, mixing with hands until crumbly. Press two-thirds of the mixture onto bottom of 10-inch (3 L) springform pan. Bake in 400°F (200° C) oven for 10 minutes or until light golden but not browned. Let cool. Press remaining mixture up sides of pan.

Filling: In heavy stainless steel saucepan, stir together rhubarb, granulated sugar, tapioca and cinnamon; let stand for 15 minutes. Stir in water and bring to boil; reduce heat to medium-low and cook, covered and stirring often, just until rhubarb is tender but not mushy, about 10 minutes. (Mixture should be quite thick.) Let cool slightly; pour into crust.

In large bowl, beat eggs until light in color; stir in sour cream, brown sugar, lemon zest and vanilla. Pour over rhubarb and bake in 350°F (180° C) oven for about 1 hour or until top is golden and custard is set. Let cool and refrigerate, covered, for at least 3 hours or overnight. Run sharp knife around outside of torte; remove edge of pan.

Garnish: Sprinkle icing sugar over torte. Sprinkle a little lemon zest in centre. Makes 8 servings.

*Increase tapioca to 1/3 cup (75 mL) if using frozen rhubarb.

THE WINE

This torte is both tart and sweet. Any dessert wine you serve with it should have good acidity. The late-harvested Riesling grape grown in cool climates (Germany, Alsace, Ontario) will be ideal.

International option: Riesling Auslese (Germany), Late Harvest Riesling from California or Oregon.

Canadian option: B.C. or Ontario Late Harvest Riesling.

A Planned Potluck Supper

Two-Bean Chili Cobbler

Peanut Crunch Chicken Thighs

Down-Home Potato Salad

*Corn and Hearts of Palm Salad
with Lime Dressing*

Creamy Cajun Coleslaw with Spiced Pecans

Glazed Cherry Cake

Mocha Pecan Pie

When a number of people get together socially and call it a potluck, this definition should extend to having people bring whatever they happen to make. But when I suggest this to a group of friends who get together every year for such a party, they get very nervous. So what if everyone brings potatoes? To me a 'planned potluck' is an oxymoron. I love potatoes anyway, and one such meal won't destroy you.

This menu is for all those who need some assurance of main course, salads or side dishes and dessert – like a real meal. It's perfect too for family reunions when your sisters-in-law ask what they can bring to your house.

It's a fun menu that's very flexible. Offer two desserts or one; skip one of the main courses or salads. Each dish will serve six to eight people by itself, but if you offer all of them, the menu will serve many more. Double the chicken recipe if you like. This casual menu will let you plan perfectly for the appetites of your family or guests.

PARTY PRIMER

1. *Up to three days ahead, make corn salad.*
2. *Up to two days ahead, prepare Two-Bean Chili.*
3. *Up to one day ahead, make Creamy Cajun Coleslaw and toast pecans.*
4. *Early in the day, make Glazed Cherry Cake. Make Mocha Pecan Pie. Make Down-Home Potato Salad.*
5. *Up to four hours ahead, prepare Peanut Crunch Chicken. Bring corn salad to room temperature.*
6. *Just before serving, make Cornmeal Biscuit Topping and bake with chili. Bake chicken. Stir pecans into coleslaw.*
7. *Whip cream to serve with pie.*

Two-Bean Chili Cobbler

1 tbsp	vegetable oil	15 mL
1/2 lb	small mushrooms	250 g
1-1/2 lb	lean ground beef	750 g
1	onion, chopped	1
2	cloves garlic, minced	2
1	jalapeño pepper (fresh or canned), seeded and minced	1
1 tbsp	chili powder	15 mL
1 tsp	ground cumin	5 mL
1/2 tsp	each dried oregano and salt	2 mL
1/4 tsp	hot pepper flakes	1 mL
1	can (28 oz/796 mL) tomatoes (undrained)	1
1	can (7-1/2 oz/213 mL) tomato sauce	1
1	each can (19 oz/540 mL) black beans and red kidney beans (or 2 kidney), drained and rinsed	1

Cornmeal Biscuit Topping:

1 cup	all-purpose flour	250 mL
3/4 cup	coarse cornmeal	175 mL
1 tsp	baking powder	5 mL
1/2 tsp	each baking soda, salt and granulated sugar	2 mL
1 cup	shredded Cheddar cheese	250 mL
3 tbsp	chopped fresh coriander	50 mL
3/4 cup	buttermilk or soured milk*	175 mL
1	egg	1
3 tbsp	vegetable oil	50 mL

This is a fairly straightforward version of everyone's favorite, with the addition of a cornmeal biscuit topping that makes it more like a finished-off casserole. If you're carrying it away, take the completed chili and ingredients for topping in two separate containers — all ready to put together just before serving.

In large ovenproof saucepan, heat oil over medium heat; cook mushrooms for 5 minutes. Remove with slotted spoon and set aside.

Add beef, onion, garlic and jalapeño pepper; cook over high heat until meat is no longer pink, about 7 minutes. Drain off any fat. Sprinkle with chili powder, cumin, oregano, salt and hot pepper flakes. Stir in tomatoes, tomato sauce, and black and red kidney beans.

Return mushrooms to pan and bring to simmer; cook, uncovered, for 45 minutes, stirring occasionally to prevent sticking. (Chili can be cooled, covered and refrigerated for up to 2 days; warm slightly on low heat before proceeding.)

Cornmeal Biscuit Topping: In large bowl, combine flour, cornmeal, baking powder, baking soda, salt and sugar; stir in cheese and coriander. Stir together buttermilk, egg and oil; add all at once to dry ingredients, stirring only enough to combine. Drop by large spoonfuls onto hot chili; bake in 425°F (220°C) oven for 15 to 20 minutes or until lightly browned and set. Makes 6 to 8 servings.

* To sour milk, combine 2 tsp (10 mL) lemon juice or vinegar with 3/4 cup (175 mL) milk and let stand for 15 minutes.

THE WINE

When you consider matching a wine to a dish, you usually zero in on the meat, fish or seafood and think about how this 'centrepiece' is prepared. But in a 'Planned Potluck Supper,' Rose has put together side dishes that compete for your palate's attention by virtue of their spiciness. Jalepeño pepper, chili, cumin, coriander, paprika, mustard, cayenne and cider vinegar make for a strong array of ingredients that would overpower most wines.

You could go with a powerful red with some sweetness (sweeter wines stand up better to spices), such as a Recioto della Amarone from Italy's Veneto region, a Zinfandel from California, or a Châteauneuf-du-Pâpe from a good year, but my preference would be a white with good acidity and lots of fruit. Chilled wine would refresh the palate.

International option: Rhine or Mosel Riesling Spätlese, Muscat or Gewürztraminer from Alsace or Australian dry Muscat.

Canadian option: Ontario or B.C. medium-dry Riesling.

Peanut Crunch Chicken Thighs

8	chicken thighs	8
1/2 cup	all-purpose flour	125 mL
1 tsp	paprika	5 mL
1/2 tsp	each salt and pepper	2 mL
Pinch	hot pepper flakes	Pinch
1 cup	dry-roasted peanuts	250 mL
1	egg	1
2 tbsp	each milk and olive oil	25 mL

Pat chicken dry. In sturdy plastic bag or bowl, stir together flour, paprika, salt, pepper and hot pepper flakes.

In food processor, chop peanuts finely, being careful not to let become a paste. Transfer to shallow bowl; toss with 2 tbsp (25 mL) of the flour mixture.

In another shallow bowl, beat egg with milk. Dredge each chicken thigh in flour mixture; dip into egg mixture, then coat evenly with peanut mixture. (Chicken can be prepared to this point, covered and refrigerated for up to 4 hours.)

In large ovenproof skillet, heat oil over medium-high heat; brown chicken well on all sides, carefully turning, 6 to 8 minutes. Transfer to 375°F (190°C) oven and bake for about 35 minutes or until juices run clear when chicken is pierced. Makes 4 to 8 servings.

These crisp oven-fried chicken thighs will be a hit with everyone, young and old.

Down-Home Potato Salad

5	potatoes	5
2 tbsp	white wine vinegar	25 mL
1 tsp	granulated sugar	5 mL
4	hard-cooked eggs, finely chopped	4
1/4 cup	each diced red onion, celery and sweet green pepper	50 mL
2	cornichons (or 1 small dill pickle), minced	2
1 cup	light mayonnaise	250 mL
1 tbsp	Dijon mustard	15 mL
Pinch	cayenne pepper	Pinch
	Salt and pepper	

Peel and quarter potatoes. In saucepan of boiling salted water, cook potatoes until tender; drain well and coarsely chop. Place in bowl and combine with vinegar and sugar while still hot.

Add eggs, onion, celery, green pepper and pickles; toss gently. Stir together mayonnaise, mustard, cayenne, and salt and

I could sit down to a big plate of this delicious salad and ask for nothing more. It does, however, go awfully well with crisp chicken.

pepper to taste; stir into potato mixture. Serve warm or cover and refrigerate for up to 8 hours; bring to room temperature to serve. Makes 6 servings.

CORN AND HEARTS OF PALM SALAD WITH LIME DRESSING

Hearts of palm add an exotic touch that turns a simple everyday salad into company fare. Sharon Boyd, my able assistant and friend, brought home the idea from a visit to France one year.

4 cups	cooked corn kernels	1 L
1 cup	sliced (1/4-inch/5 mm) hearts of palm	250 mL
1/4 cup	diced sweet red pepper	50 mL
1/4 cup	diced white onion	50 mL

Lime Dressing:

2 tbsp	fresh lime juice	25 mL
1 tsp	chili powder	5 mL
1/2 tsp	finely grated lime zest	2 mL
	Salt and pepper	
1/3 cup	olive oil	75 mL
	Spinach or lettuce leaves (optional)	

In large bowl, stir together corn, hearts of palm, red pepper and onion.

Lime Dressing: In small bowl, stir together lime juice, chili powder, lime zest, and salt and pepper to taste; gradually whisk in oil. Gently stir into corn mixture. Serve immediately or cover and refrigerate for up to 3 days. Bring to room temperature to serve.

To serve, transfer to pretty glass bowl or mound on platter lined with spinach leaves. Makes 6 servings.

Creamy Cajun Coleslaw with Spiced Pecans

1/2 cup	coarsely chopped pecans	125 mL
1/4 tsp	each cayenne pepper, black pepper, dried thyme, basil and oregano	1 mL
2	cloves garlic, minced	2
Half	head cabbage, finely shredded (about 10 cups/2.5 L)	Half
1/2 cup	each diced white onion and seedless raisins	125 mL
3/4 cup	light mayonnaise	175 mL
3 tbsp	cider vinegar	50 mL
2 tbsp	brown grainy mustard Salt and pepper	25 mL

Mix pecans, cayenne, pepper, thyme, basil, oregano and garlic. In skillet, toast mixture over medium-low heat for 10 minutes or until fragrant, stirring often. Set aside.

In bowl, toss together cabbage, onion and raisins. Stir together mayonnaise, vinegar, mustard, and salt and pepper to taste; add to cabbage and toss well. Cover and refrigerate for at least 3 hours or up to 24 hours. Just before serving, gently stir in spiced pecans. Makes 6 servings.

I love the various textures and flavors in this easy cabbage salad that's enlivened with a few nuts and raisins.

Glazed Cherry Cake

Topping:		
1/3 cup	packed brown sugar	75 mL
2 tbsp	all-purpose flour	25 mL
1 tsp	ground cinnamon	5 mL
1/4 cup	butter	50 mL
Cake:		
1/4 cup	butter, at room temperature	50 mL
1 cup	granulated sugar	250 mL
2	eggs, separated	2
1 tsp	vanilla	5 mL
1-1/2 cups	all-purpose flour	375 mL
1 tsp	baking powder	5 mL
1/4 tsp	salt	1 mL
1/2 cup	milk	125 mL
2 cups	drained pitted red cherries	500 mL
Glaze:		
3/4 cup	icing sugar	175 mL
1 tbsp	milk	15 mL
1/2 tsp	almond extract	2 mL

This easy-to-make and easy-to-carry cake will be a hit with everyone. It's terrific warm, but leftover cake keeps fresh and moist for a couple of days. If using frozen cherries, thaw first and drain well.

Topping: In medium bowl, stir together sugar, flour and cinnamon; cut in butter until crumbly. Set aside.

Cake: In large bowl, cream butter with sugar; beat in egg yolks, one at a time, until light and fluffy. Stir in vanilla. In separate bowl, beat egg whites until stiff; set aside. Sift or stir together flour, baking powder and salt; add alternately with milk to creamed mixture. Fold in egg whites.

Spread batter in greased 9-inch (2.5 L) square cake pan. Scatter cherries on top. Sprinkle with topping. Bake in 350°F (180°C) oven for about 45 minutes or until tester inserted in centre comes out clean.

Glaze: Meanwhile, in small bowl, stir together icing sugar, milk and almond extract; drizzle over hot cake. Cut into squares to serve. Makes 9 to 12 servings.

Mocha Pecan Pie

This variation on pecan pie is perfect for company and not overly sweet. Serve at room temperature with softly whipped cream.

6 oz	bittersweet or semisweet chocolate	175 g
1/4 cup	coffee liqueur	50 mL
1 tbsp	instant coffee granules	15 mL
1/2 cup	packed brown sugar	125 mL
1 cup	corn syrup	250 mL
3	eggs, beaten	3
1/4 cup	butter, melted	50 mL
2 tsp	vanilla	10 mL
1/4 tsp	salt	1 mL
1 cup	coarsely chopped pecans	250 mL
1	unbaked 9-inch (23 cm) pie shell	1
1 cup	pecan halves	250 mL
	Slightly sweetened whipped cream	

In heatproof bowl set over simmering water, melt chocolate with coffee liqueur and coffee granules, stirring until smooth. Remove from heat and stir in brown sugar until dissolved. Stir in corn syrup, eggs, butter, vanilla, salt and chopped pecans. Pour into pie shell and arrange pecan halves on top.

Bake in 350°F (180°C) oven for 45 to 50 minutes or until edges are set and centre still jiggles slightly. Cool on rack. Serve each wedge with dollop of softly whipped cream. Makes 8 servings.

The Wine

Asti Spumante goes beautifully with cake. For the pie, I would suggest a Cream Sherry.

AN ELEGANT MIDSUMMER BARBECUE FOR FOUR

Bruschetta with Two-Tomato Relish

Rosemary-Grilled Veal Chops

Oven-Roasted Potato Wedges

Roasted Ratatouille

Green Salad

Plum Clafouti with Cognac Cream

*T*his is such a colorful and delicious meal that I prepare it often. Because it's one of the easiest in the book and so quick to put together, it's perfect for a Saturday night meal when you are entertaining special weekend guests or when you decide to have friends over at the end of a busy week.

PARTY PRIMER

1. *Up to five days ahead, make Roasted Ratatouille.*
2. *Up to four hours ahead, prepare Two-Tomato Relish. Marinate veal chops.*
3. *Up to two hours ahead, make Cognac Cream for Clafouti.*
4. *Prepare and cook Potato Wedges.*
5. *Prepare Clafouti to pop into the oven when Wedges are cooked.*
6. *While barbecue is getting hot enough for chops, grill bread for Bruschetta and serve with relish. Grill chops.*

Bruschetta with Two Tomato Relish

2	medium tomatoes	2
2 tbsp	finely chopped (oil-packed) sun-dried tomatoes	25 mL
2	cloves garlic, minced	2
1 tbsp	chopped fresh basil (or 1 tsp/5 mL dried)	15 mL
1 tbsp	oil from sun-dried tomatoes	15 mL
Pinch	dried oregano	Pinch
	Salt and pepper	
1	small baguette	1
1	clove garlic, halved	1
2 tbsp	extra-virgin olive oil	25 mL

The perfect appetizer for a barbecued supper, bruschetta is Italian garlic bread made with olive oil instead of butter. This one has a zesty topping of a fresh-and-dried tomato relish. The relish can be made ahead, but the bread slices are best served hot from the grill.

Seed and finely dice tomatoes; place in sieve to drain for 30 minutes.

In bowl, combine diced tomatoes, sun-dried tomatoes, minced garlic, basil, oil, oregano, and salt and pepper to taste. (Relish can be covered and refrigerated for up to 4 hours.)

Cut bread into 1/2-inch (1 cm) thick slices to make 20 to 24 slices. Lightly grill on each side over medium-high heat. While still hot, rub one side with cut side of garlic; spoon some relish over top. Sprinkle with grinding of pepper; drizzle with olive oil. Makes 4 servings.

The Wine

The key word here is *elegant* which suggests fine wines to accompany the three courses. Since it is midsummer and presumably a warm evening, you don't want to serve full-bodied reds with the meat course (which you might consider for a winter dinner).

The tomato in the Bruschetta is very acidic and cries out for a wine with good acidity. To stand up to the garlic, the wine must have lots of flavor. So I am suggesting a rosé from the southern Rhône which would look good in the glass.

International option: Tavel or Lirac rosé (Rhône) or any Provence or Languedoc rosé.

Canadian option: Ontario dry rosé or B.C. Pinot Blanc.

ROSEMARY-GRILLED VEAL CHOPS

When I want to serve something that's fast and easy but a bit on the elegant side for company, I do these chops.

4	thick veal loin chops	4
1/3 cup	dry white wine	75 mL
1/4 cup	olive oil	50 mL
1 tbsp	chopped fresh rosemary (or 1 tsp/5 mL crumbled dried)	15 mL
1/2 tsp	grated lemon zest	2 mL
	Salt and pepper	

Place chops in glass dish just big enough to hold them in single layer. Whisk together wine, oil, rosemary and lemon zest; pour over chops. Cover and marinate at room temperature for 30 minutes or up to 4 hours in refrigerator. Remove from refrigerator 30 minutes before grilling.

Sprinkle with salt and pepper. Place on greased grill over medium-high heat; grill for 5 to 10 minutes per side, depending on thickness, or until desired doneness. Makes 4 servings.

THE WINE

The white wine should have a touch of acidity to bring out the flavor of the rosemary in the veal.

International option: Puligny-Montrachet (Burgundy) or New Zealand Chardonnay or Pinot Grigio (Friuli, Northern Italy).

Canadian option: Ontario Chardonnay.

Single white option: White Burgundy.

OVEN-ROASTED POTATO WEDGES

3	large baking potatoes, well scrubbed	3
1/2 tsp	paprika	2 mL
1 tbsp	vegetable oil	15 mL
	Salt	

Place baking sheet in oven and preheat to 450°F (230°C). Cut each potato lengthwise into 12 wedges. In bowl, toss potatoes with paprika. Sprinkle with oil and toss again.

Spread out in single layer on hot sheet. Bake for 15 minutes; turn wedges over and bake for 10 to 15 minutes longer or until crisp and golden brown. Sprinkle with salt to taste. Serve immediately. Makes 4 servings.

Crisp on the outside and moist in the centre, these easy low-fat wedges will appeal to the most discriminating potato aficionado.

ROASTED RATATOUILLE

1	medium eggplant	1
	Salt	
1	each sweet red and yellow pepper	1
	Olive oil	
1	small Spanish onion, halved	1
	Pepper	
2	cloves garlic, minced	2
1	can (7-1/2 oz/213 mL) tomato sauce	1
2 tbsp	dry sherry	25 mL
1 tbsp	each soy sauce and red wine vinegar	15 mL
1 tsp	granulated sugar	5 mL
Pinch	hot pepper flakes	Pinch

Peel eggplant; cut crosswise into 1/2-inch (1 cm) thick slices. Sprinkle lightly with salt and set aside.

Roast peppers on grill, under broiler, or in 450°F (230°C) oven for about 15 minutes, turning often, until blistered and charred all over. Place under overturned bowl for 10 minutes; peel, seed and cut into 1/2-inch (1 cm) chunks.

Rinse eggplant and pat dry. Brush with oil and grill over medium-high heat for 10 to 15 minutes or until golden brown and softened, turning once. (Do not char.) Cut into 1/2-inch (1 cm) dice.

Brush onion with oil; sprinkle with salt and pepper to taste. Grill for about 20 minutes, turning often, or until very tender. Remove any charred outside skin; cut into 1/2-inch (1 cm) dice.

In large skillet, heat 1 tsp (5 mL) oil over medium heat; cook garlic for 2 minutes. Stir in peppers, onion, tomato sauce, sherry,

This tasty vegetable stew gains even more flavor from roasting and grilling the vegetables before they are combined in an unusual vinaigrette.

soy sauce, vinegar, sugar and hot pepper flakes. Cook, stirring, for 5 minutes or until thickened. Stir in eggplant. (Ratatouille can be cooled, covered and refrigerated for up to 5 days.) Serve at room temperature or reheat. Makes 4 servings.

Plum Clafouti with Cognac Cream

When I want something elegant but quick, I enjoy serving a fruit dessert like this one. A kind of custard or thick fruit pancake from Limousin, France, clafouti (also spelled with an 's,' clafoutis, in both singular and plural) was originally made with black cherries. I love the look of it with purple plums, but use whatever fruit is in season, varying the liqueur to complement the fruit and adjusting the sugar to the fruit's sweetness.

2 cups	halved pitted purple prune plums (about 10)	500 mL
1/2 cup	granulated sugar	125 mL
1 tbsp	kirsch or brandy	15 mL
1-1/4 cups	light cream	300 mL
2	eggs	2
2 tbsp	all-purpose flour	25 mL
Pinch	salt	Pinch
1/2 tsp	vanilla	2 mL
	Icing sugar	

Cognac Cream:

1/2 cup	whipping cream	125 mL
1 tbsp	each cognac or brandy and icing sugar	15 mL

Toss plums with 2 tbsp (25 mL) of the sugar and kirsch. Set aside.

Butter 6-cup (1.5 L) shallow pretty baking dish; sprinkle with 1 tbsp (15 mL) of the sugar.

In blender or food processor, blend light cream, eggs, flour and salt for 1 minute. Add remaining sugar and vanilla; blend a few seconds longer.

Arrange plums, cut side down, and their juice in prepared dish; pour egg mixture over top. Bake in 375°F (190°C) oven for about 45 minutes or until well puffed and golden. Let cool until barely warm. Sprinkle with icing sugar.

Cognac Cream: Meanwhile, whip cream, cognac and icing sugar. Serve with clafouti. Makes 4 servings.

The Wine

The sweetness of this dessert requires a very sweet wine to accompany it, otherwise it will make the wine taste acidic. The addition of brandy to the cream means that a delicate dessert wine would be overpowered.

International option: Marsala or Australian Muscat Liqueur or Italian dessert Malvasia.

SUMMER MARKET SUPPER FOR SIX

Chilled Cucumber Soup with Walnuts

Grilled Beef Tenderloin with Red Pepper Sauce

Roasted New Potatoes and Garlic

Savory Green and Yellow Beans

Buttered Pattypan Squash

Iced Tomato Salad

Cherry Crème Brûlée

Chocolate Macaroons

Assorted Fresh Fruit and Coffee

This elegant but simple supper depends on a trip to the market when fruits and vegetables are at their summer best. When produce is fresh and good, there's no need to spend hours in the kitchen.

In fact, although much of this dinner can be prepared one or two days in advance, the dishes are so quick and easy that you might go shopping Saturday morning (especially if that's the day of your farmers' market) and prepare everything for the evening meal after returning home.

PARTY PRIMER

1. Up to five days ahead, make Chocolate Macaroons.
2. Up to two days ahead, make Chilled Cucumber Soup. Make custards for crème brûlée and cook cherries.
3. Up to one day ahead, prepare Red Pepper Sauce.
4. Early in the day, blanch green and yellow beans.
5. Four hours ahead, marinate beef. Precook pattypan squash.
6. Up to three hours ahead, prepare new potatoes.
7. Up to one hour ahead, make Tomato Salad.
8. Roast potatoes.
9. Grill beef. Reheat and finish beans and squash.
10. Just before serving, top Tomato Salad with ice and garnish with basil.
11. Just before serving, finish and broil Crème Brûlée.

Chilled Cucumber Soup with Walnuts

3	medium field cucumbers (about 1-1/2 lb/750 g)	3
	Salt	
2 cups	buttermilk	500 mL
2	cloves garlic	2
1	small onion, chopped	1
1/4 cup	chopped fresh parsley	50 mL
1 tbsp	minced fresh chives	15 mL
1 cup	each plain yogurt and light sour cream	250 mL
1 tbsp	fresh lemon juice	15 mL
1 tbsp	granulated sugar	15 mL
	White pepper	
Pinch	cayenne pepper	Pinch
1/2 cup	toasted finely chopped walnuts	125 mL
	Borage blossoms, snipped chives or parsley sprigs	

This easy-to-make soup is a refreshing start to any summer meal. If borage blossoms (the pretty purple-blue star-shaped flowers of the herb) are available, they make a perfect garnish.

Peel cucumbers and slice in half lengthwise. With teaspoon, scoop out seeds and discard. Chop cucumbers coarsely; transfer to sieve. Sprinkle lightly with salt and let stand for 30 minutes.

Drain cucumbers and pat dry. Place in blender along with buttermilk, garlic, onion, parsley and chives; purée until smooth.

Transfer to large bowl; stir in yogurt, sour cream, lemon juice, sugar, salt and white pepper to taste and cayenne. Stir in walnuts. Cover and chill for at least 1 hour or for up to 2 days

Serve in chilled bowls garnished with borage blossoms. Makes 6 servings.

THE WINE

I don't recommend any wine with such a delicate soup but for the inveterate wine drinker, I might suggest a chilled Manzanilla sherry. It's very dry.

GRILLED BEEF TENDERLOIN WITH RED PEPPER SAUCE

Tenderloin steaks take very little time to prepare and only a few minutes to grill to fork-tenderness.

3 lb	beef tenderloin roast	1.5 kg
2	cloves garlic, minced	2
2/3 cup	dry red wine	150 mL
2 tbsp	olive oil	25 mL
1/3 cup	packed fresh rosemary sprigs	75 mL
	(or 4 tsp/20 mL dried rosemary)	
2	large sweet red peppers	2
1 tbsp	balsamic vinegar	15 mL
	(or red wine vinegar and pinch sugar)	
	Salt and pepper	
	Fresh rosemary sprigs	

Cut roast against the grain into six 1-inch (2.5 cm) thick steaks; place in shallow glass dish just big enough to hold in single layer. Sprinkle with half of the garlic, the wine, olive oil and rosemary. Cover and marinate in refrigerator for 4 hours, turning occasionally. Remove from refrigerator 30 minutes before grilling.

Meanwhile, roast red peppers under broiler, on grill, or in 450° F (230° C) oven for about 15 minutes, turning often, until blistered and charred. Remove and place under overturned bowl to steam for 10 minutes. Peel and seed, catching any juices. Purée in blender along with remaining garlic, vinegar, salt and pepper to taste and any juices. (Sauce can be covered and refrigerated for up to 1 day.) Pour into saucepan; heat gently to serve.

Pat steaks dry and sprinkle with salt and pepper. Grill on greased grill over high heat for about 3 minutes per side. Serve on hot plates with pepper sauce spooned alongside or over top. Garnish with rosemary sprigs. Makes 6 servings.

THE WINE

The bite of the red pepper sauce calls for a red wine with a touch of tannin and a peppery finish.

International option: A good Rhône red (Crozes-Hermitage, Châteauneuf-du-Pâpe) or California Zinfandel or Australian Shiraz.

Canadian option: Ontario Baco Noir.

White wine option: White Rhône (Châteauneuf-du-Pâpe) or white Mâcon from Southern Burgundy (Pouilly-Fuissé, St. Véran).

ROASTED NEW POTATOES AND GARLIC

3 lb	small new potatoes (about 24), unpeeled	1.5 kg
18	cloves garlic	18
2 tbsp	olive oil	25 mL
	Coarse salt and pepper	

Scrub potatoes and dry. In small roasting pan, toss together potatoes, garlic and oil. Sprinkle with salt and pepper to taste. (Potatoes can be set aside for up to 3 hours.)

Cover and roast in 375°F (190°C) oven until tender, 30 to 40 minutes, stirring occasionally. Makes 6 servings.

Both waxy new potatoes and garlic become incredibly sweet with this simple method of cooking.

SAVORY GREEN AND YELLOW BEANS

3/4 lb	each green beans and wax beans	375 g
2 tbsp	butter	25 mL
	Salt and pepper	
1 tbsp	minced fresh savory	15 mL
	(or 1 tsp/5 mL crushed dried)	

Trim beans by removing just stem end. In large saucepan of boiling salted water, cook beans, uncovered, for 4 to 5 minutes or until just tender. Drain and refresh under cold running water. (Beans can be wrapped in tea towel and refrigerated for up to 8 hours.)

In large skillet, melt butter over medium heat. Add beans and shake pan to coat; season with salt and pepper to taste. Cover and cook for 2 to 3 minutes or until heated through. Sprinkle with savory. Makes 6 servings.

When slender yellow, or wax, beans are in season, they make a pretty and simple presentation with green beans of the same size.

Buttered Pattypan Squash

2 lb	pattypan squash	1 kg
2 tbsp	butter	25 mL
	Salt and pepper	

In saucepan, place squash in steamer basket over boiling water; steam for 4 to 5 minutes or until just tender when pierced with tip of knife.

In saucepan, melt butter; add squash and toss to coat. (Squash can be prepared to this point, covered and set aside for up to 4 hours. Heat gently for about 5 minutes or until squash is heated through and tender.) Season with salt and pepper to taste. Makes 6 servings.

If you can buy baby pattypan squash (pale green scalloped squashes), they make interesting shapes on the plates. Cut bigger ones into halves or quarters.

Iced Tomato Salad

6	large ripe tomatoes	6
1 tbsp	chopped fresh basil	15 mL
2	cloves garlic, minced	2
1/4 cup	extra-virgin olive oil	50 mL
1 tbsp	balsamic vinegar	15 mL
Pinch	granulated sugar	Pinch
	Salt and pepper	
6	ice cubes	6
	Sprigs fresh basil	

Tomatoes and basil have long been a favorite duo, but the addition of sweet balsamic vinegar and ice cubes make this a sparkling and refreshing salad indeed.

Slice tomatoes into thin wedges; place in large shallow bowl. Sprinkle with chopped basil. Stir together garlic, oil, vinegar, sugar, and salt and pepper to taste; pour over tomatoes. Let stand for at least 10 minutes and up to 1 hour.

To serve, place ice cubes on top; garnish with basil sprigs. Makes 6 servings.

CHERRY CRÈME BRÛLÉE

1-1/2 cups	whipping cream	375 mL
1/4 cup	milk	50 mL
4	egg yolks	4
1/3 cup	granulated sugar	75 mL
1 tsp	vanilla	5 mL
2 cups	pitted sweet cherries	500 mL
1 tbsp	raw (Demerara) sugar or golden brown sugar	15 mL

Elegant and so easy, these little custards are very appealing with their creaminess and crunchy fruit topping.

In small heavy saucepan, heat cream and milk until bubbles just start to form around outside. Remove from heat. In bowl, slightly whisk egg yolks with granulated sugar just to combine; do not let foam. Very gradually pour in hot cream mixture, stirring constantly. Stir in vanilla.

Strain through fine sieve into pitcher or measuring cup. Pour into six 1/2-cup (125 mL) heatproof ramekins. Place in baking pan just big enough to hold them; pour hot water into pan to come two-thirds up sides of ramekins.

Cover with foil; bake in 325°F (160°C) oven for about 25 minutes or until custards are just set but still jiggly in centres. Remove ramekins to cool on rack; refrigerate, covered, until very cold, at least 6 hours and up to 2 days.

In heavy saucepan, bring cherries to boil over medium heat; cover, reduce heat to low and cook for 5 to 8 minutes or until tender but still hold their shape. Cool completely; cover and chill for up to 2 days.

Just before serving, top cold custards with cherries and their juices. Sprinkle each with 1 tsp (5 mL) raw sugar. Broil on rack nearest heat for about 3-1/2 minutes or until sugar melts, bubbles and caramelizes. Watch carefully; do not let cherries burn. Serve immediately. Makes 6 servings.

CHOCOLATE MACAROONS

1 cup	granulated sugar	250 mL
1/3 cup	unsweetened cocoa powder	75 mL
3	egg whites	3
Pinch	salt	Pinch
1 tsp	vanilla	5 mL
2 cups	unsweetened desiccated coconut	500 mL

These super-easy cookies, which are not overly sweet, are delicious with the creamy custard and fruit.

Stir sugar and cocoa together until smooth. In bowl, beat egg whites with salt until stiff peaks form. On low speed, gradually beat in sugar mixture. Add vanilla; fold in coconut.

Line 3 baking sheets with foil. Drop mixture 1 inch (2.5 cm) apart onto sheets. Bake in 325°F (160°C) oven for 15 to 17 minutes or until dry outside but still soft inside. With spatula, carefully transfer to racks to cool. (Macaroons can be stored in airtight container for up to 5 days.) Makes about 4 dozen.

THE WINE

The velvety custard of the Cherry Crème Brûlée marries well with sweet wines that have a good balance of acidity.

International option: Tokay Aszu (Hungary) or Vin Santo (Italy).

Canadian option: Late Harvest Riesling.

A HARVEST SUPPER FOR SIX

Ginger Squash Soup

Zucchini and Tomato Tart

*Grilled Lamb Loins with Roasted Pepper
and Garlic Sauce*

Pear Potato Salad

Steamed Buttered Broccoli

Fall Fruits with Mascarpone Cups

*V*elvety soup, a colorful vegetable tart, smoky grilled lamb with a zesty sauce, an unusual side salad of potatoes and pears, plain broccoli steamed until just bright green and a juicy selection of fall fruit served with cheese and liqueur — all combine for a menu that looks spectacular, has great flavors and is easy to put together. Most of the dishes can be made ahead; the rest cook quickly for a supper you will note as one to serve at least annually.

PARTY PRIMER

1. *Up to two days ahead, make Roasted Pepper and Garlic Sauce.*
2. *Up to one day ahead, prepare Ginger Squash Soup. Make and pre-bake crust for Zucchini and Tomato Tart.*
3. *Up to eight hours ahead, prepare Pear Potato Salad if serving cold or at room temperature.*
4. *Up to six hours ahead, arrange mascarpone cups on plates and refrigerate. Marinate lamb loins.*
5. *Several hours ahead, prepare filling for tart and refrigerate.*
6. *Just before serving, finish tart and bake.*
7. *Add cream to soup and reheat gently.*
8. *Prepare salad if serving warm.*
9. *Grill lamb and reheat sauce.*
10. *Steam broccoli.*
11. *Arrange fruit on dessert plates and add liqueur.*

GINGER SQUASH SOUP

1	acorn squash (about 2-1/2 lb/1.25 kg)	1
2 tbsp	butter	25 mL
2	leeks, thinly sliced	2
1	small carrot, thinly sliced	1
4 cups	chicken stock	1 L
1 tsp	ground ginger	5 mL
1/2 tsp	salt	2 mL
1/4 tsp	pepper	1 mL
1/2 cup	light cream or milk	125 mL
	Sour cream	
	Snipped chives or sliced green onion tops	

A small bowl of this smooth soup will pique appetites at any fall dinner party. You can use any winter squash, cutting it into large pieces. Baking or microwaving the squash instead of boiling it helps retain all the flavor. Slowly cooking the leeks over low heat releases their sweetness.

Cut squash in half and remove seeds; place, cut side down, in shallow glass baking dish. Cover with vented plastic wrap and microwave at High for 8 to 10 minutes or until tender. Let stand for 5 minutes. (Alternatively, cover and bake in 350°F/180°C oven for 40 minutes or until tender.) Scrape squash from skin.

Meanwhile, in large saucepan, melt butter over low heat; cook leeks and carrot, uncovered and stirring occasionally, for about 40 minutes or until leeks are softened and lightly browned.

Stir in stock, cooked squash, ginger, salt and pepper; cover and simmer over medium heat for 20 minutes. Transfer to food processor or blender and purée until smooth; return to saucepan. (Recipe can be prepared to this point, covered and refrigerated for up to 24 hours.)

Stir in cream and gently heat through but do not boil. Taste and adjust seasoning, if necessary. Garnish each serving with swirl of sour cream and sprinkling of chives. Makes 6 servings.

THE WINE

The predominant flavor in the soup is ginger, enriched with butter and cream. It isn't necessary to have a wine with this dish, but in the spirit of Thanksgiving, why not try a glass.

International option: Palo Cortado sherry or Sercial (dry Madeira) served at cellar temperature (50° - 55° F/ 10° - 12° C).

Canadian option: Ontario Late Harvest Gewürztraminer.

Zucchini and Tomato Tart

This pretty vegetable tart looks spectacular, but is very easy to make. The tart shell can be made up to one day ahead.

	Pastry for 11-inch (28 cm) single-crust pie	
3	eggs	3
2 cups	shredded Gruyère cheese	500 mL
1/2 tsp	salt	2 mL
1/4 tsp	pepper	1 mL
2	cloves garlic, minced	2
1	small zucchini	1
2	small plum tomatoes	2
	Olive oil	
1/2 tsp	each dried basil and oregano	2 mL

On lightly floured surface, roll out pastry and line tart tin (preferably with removable bottom). Prick bottom with fork; line with parchment paper or foil. Fill with dried beans or rice; bake in 400°F (200°C) oven for 5 minutes. Reduce heat to 350°F (180°C) and bake for 10 to 15 minutes or until golden. Remove paper and beans; bake 5 minutes longer. Cool.

In blender or food processor, combine eggs, cheese, salt, pepper and garlic; spread in prepared crust.

Cut zucchini in half lengthwise and thinly slice crosswise. Thinly slice tomatoes. Arrange decoratively on top of cheese mixture, overlapping slices and alternating vegetables. Brush with oil; sprinkle with basil and oregano. Bake in 375°F (190°C) oven for about 30 minutes or until knife inserted in centre comes out clean and tart is golden brown. Cut into wedges and serve hot. Makes 6 servings.

The Wine

The best grape to accompany vegetables is the Sauvignon Blanc, especially if they are as acidic as tomatoes.

International option: Sancerre (Loire) or Sonoma Valley Fumé Blanc (California).

Canadian option: Ontario Seyval Blanc or dry Vidal.

Grilled Lamb Loins with Roasted Pepper and Garlic Sauce

2 lb	boneless lamb loins	1 kg
2 tbsp	olive oil	25 mL
4 tsp	fresh lemon juice	20 mL
1	small clove garlic, minced	1
	Pepper	

Roasted Pepper and Garlic Sauce:

1	head garlic	1
2 tsp	olive oil	10 mL
3	small sweet red peppers	3
Half	small hot red chili pepper	Half
1	small onion, halved	1
1/2 cup	whipping cream	125 mL
1/2 tsp	granulated sugar	2 mL
1/4 tsp	salt	1 mL

The delicate flavor of lamb could easily be overpowered by assertive flavoring agents, so try just a hint of mesquite, rosemary, spices or grapevine clippings on the hot coals.

This recipe makes a very generous amount of red pepper sauce, but any leftover sauce is delicious served as a dip for crudités or as a sauce for pasta.

Place lamb in sturdy plastic bag set in bowl. Stir together oil, lemon juice, garlic, and pepper to taste; pour over lamb. Close bag tightly; squeeze gently to coat lamb well. Refrigerate for at least 4 hours or up to 6 hours, turning bag occasionally. Remove from refrigerator 30 minutes before grilling.

Roasted Pepper and Garlic Sauce: Remove any papery layers from garlic head. Place garlic on piece of foil; drizzle with oil and wrap loosely. Grill on coolest spot of medium-hot grill for 10 minutes. Add red and chili peppers and onion to centre of grill; grill, turning occasionally, until lightly charred, 20 to 25 minutes. Remove garlic when soft.

Remove peppers and place under overturned bowl to steam for 10 minutes; peel and seed. Remove charred leaves from onion. In food processor, combine peppers with onion. Squeeze pulp out of garlic head into processor; process until smooth. Add cream, sugar and salt; process until blended. Transfer to stainless steel saucepan. (Sauce can be covered and refrigerated for up to 2 days.)

Grill lamb on greased grill over medium-high heat, basting often with marinade and turning once when red juices pool on top, for 3 to 5 minutes per side or until meat feels springy and is still pink in centre. Cover with foil and let stand for 10 to 15 minutes before slicing thinly on diagonal.

Meanwhile, heat sauce over low heat, stirring often. Arrange slices of lamb on warm plates; spoon a little sauce onto each and pass remainder in sauceboat. Makes 6 servings.

A very spicy dish like the lamb calls for a red wine with good fruit and lively acidity. That means a young wine.

International option: Château-bottled St. Emilion or Pomerol (Bordeaux) or young Rioja red (Spain).

Canadian option: Ontario Merlot.

Single white wine option throughout the meal: Pouilly-Fumé (Loire).

PEAR POTATO SALAD

This salad, inspired by Four Seasons Restaurant in New York City, is quite different and wonderful with sausage or smoked pork chops as well as grilled lamb.

4	potatoes (unpeeled)	4
2	pears	2
3 tbsp	white vinegar	50 mL
1/2 tsp	each salt, pepper and granulated sugar	2 mL
1	clove garlic, minced	1
1/3 cup	olive oil	75 mL
	Lettuce	

Scrub potatoes. In saucepan of boiling salted water, cook potatoes for about 30 minutes or until tender but not mushy. Drain and let cool enough to handle; peel and slice into large bowl. Peel pears and thinly slice, removing cores. Toss with potatoes.

In small bowl, whisk together vinegar, salt, pepper, sugar and garlic; gradually whisk in oil. Pour over potato mixture; toss gently to coat, trying not to break slices. Serve warm, at room temperature or chilled mounded in lettuce-lined bowl or platter. Makes 6 servings.

FALL FRUITS WITH MASCARPONE CUPS

6 oz	mascarpone	175 g
1 tbsp	icing sugar	15 mL
1/4 cup	Amaretto liqueur	50 mL
	Selection of sliced or halved fruit	
	Fresh lemon juice	

In small bowl, cream mascarpone with icing sugar; blend in 1 tbsp (15 mL) of the liqueur. Mound on each of six dessert plates; swirl into rounds and make hollow in centre of each with spoon. Refrigerate for up to 6 hours.

To serve, fill hollows with remaining liqueur. Arrange fruit around mounds; sprinkle with lemon juice. Serve immediately. Makes 6 servings.

Encourage guests to have some of the cheese and liqueur with each piece of fruit. Use any kind of fruit that you find appealing in the fall market — pears, plums, cantaloupe, grapes, apples, figs. Use any liqueur you find complementary to the fruit you choose, such as Calvados, pear liqueur, Frangelico.

THE WINE

Since you are already having liqueur blended into the mascarpone cheese, a wine would be redundant. But a glass of chilled Mirabelle (golden plum eau-de-vie) would be a wonderful way to highlight the contrasting textures of the fruit and mascarpone.

FOOD PREPARATION HINTS

Green Salads:

To prepare salad greens ahead, wash and dry them well. Wrap loosely in paper towels and place in a plastic bag or large plastic container in the refrigerator for up to two days.

After you tear the greens and toss them together in a salad bowl (without the dressing), cover with a damp tea towel and refrigerate for up to two hours.

Toasting Nuts:

You'll see lots of references to toasted nuts in my recipes. I find this step is well worth the few minutes it takes because of the flavor it adds. First of all, always taste nuts before using them in a recipe. If they're rancid, they'll spoil your whole dish. Throw them out and replace them with fresh nuts. Toast nuts by spreading out on a baking sheet and baking in 350° F (180° C) oven until golden brown and fragrant, 5 to 12 minutes depending on size and kind of nut. Watch them carefully.

Crème Fraîche:

This cultured heavy cream is occasionally available for sale in plastic tubs in the dairy counter. If you cannot find it, sometimes a good sour cream can be used. Or make your own crème fraîche by whisking together equal quantities of whipping cream and sour cream; cover and refrigerate a day or two or until thickened. It will keep in the refrigerator for two weeks.

A Small Thanksgiving or Harvest Supper for Four

Warm Red Cabbage and Chèvre Salad

Cornish Hens Roasted with Pears

*Uncooked Cranberry Relish
with Citrus and Fresh Ginger*

Creamy Mashed Potatoes

Squash and Carrot Purée

Buttered Green Beans

Coconut Pumpkin Pie

*I*f your Thanksgiving table will not embrace all the aunts, uncles and cousins, and there are just three or four of you gathered together to give thanks for fall's bounty, this is the perfect menu. It's 'downscale' in size but upscale in flavor.

PARTY PRIMER

1. *Up to two weeks ahead, make Cranberry Relish.*
2. *Up to two days ahead, prepare Squash and Carrot Purée.*
3. *Several hours ahead, make and bake Coconut Pumpkin Pie.*
4. *A few hours ahead, prepare cabbage salad.*
5. *About one hour ahead, prepare and roast cornish hens. Peel potatoes and trim beans.*
6. *Just before mealtime, cook vegetables. Reheat purée. Whip cream for pie. Heat dressing and toss with salad.*

Warm Red Cabbage and Chèvre Salad

Half	small head red cabbage	Half
1/4 cup	red wine vinegar	50 mL
1/2 lb	side bacon, diced	250 g
2 tbsp	well-drained capers	25 mL
1/4 cup	vegetable oil	50 mL
2	cloves garlic, minced	2
1/4 tsp	pepper	1 mL
1 cup	crumbled soft unripened goat cheese (6 oz/175 g)	250 mL

Serve this colorful and interesting salad as a first course, or serve another time as a main luncheon course with crusty rolls. Use Greek feta or a blue cheese if goat cheese is not available.

Remove core from cabbage; shred cabbage and place in large bowl. Sprinkle with 2 tbsp (25 mL) of the vinegar and set aside.

In large skillet, fry bacon until crisp. With slotted spoon, remove bacon to drain on paper towels. Sprinkle bacon and capers over cabbage.

Pour off all but 1/4 cup (50 mL) drippings from pan; stir in oil, garlic, pepper and remaining vinegar. (Recipe can be prepared to this point and set aside for up to 3 hours.) Heat dressing until hot; pour over cabbage and toss well. Sprinkle with goat cheese. Serve immediately. Makes 4 generous appetizers.

The Wine

This is a menu for lovers of white wines because it offers a magnificent range of flavors and complementary taste sensations.

The predominating flavor of the salad is the goat cheese which needs a powerful and acidic white made from the Sauvignon Blanc grape to tame it and to stand up to the red wine vinegar.

International option: Sancerre (Loire) or New Zealand Sauvignon Blanc.

Canadian option: Ontario Seyval Blanc.

Cornish Hens Roasted with Pears

Tree-ripened pears are perfect as totable desserts and accompaniments to after-dinner cheese, but have you ever tasted how delightful they are sautéed or roasted? Sauté slices to garnish roast pork or veal; or bake quarters alongside these juicy Cornish hens.

2	Cornish hens (about 2 lb/1 kg each)	2
	Salt and pepper	
2 tbsp	butter	25 mL
1 tbsp	vegetable oil	15 mL
4	shallots (or 1 small onion), minced	4
3	pears, peeled, cored and quartered	3
1/4 cup	red port	50 mL
1 cup	chicken stock	250 mL
1 tbsp	red currant jelly	15 mL
1 tbsp	cornstarch	15 mL
	Watercress	

Wipe hens and dry well. With poultry shears or heavy cleaver, cut hens in half, cutting down each side of back bone and discarding it. Dry halves again. Sprinkle all over with salt and pepper.

In large skillet, melt butter with oil over medium-high heat; brown hen halves all over (in batches if necessary) for about 10 minutes. Transfer to roasting pan. Add shallots and pears to skillet; sauté for 3 minutes, then add to hens. Roast, uncovered, in 375°F (190°C) oven for 30 to 45 minutes or until juices run clear when thighs are pierced, basting hens and turning pears once.

Just before hens are done, pour off fat from skillet; add port and bring to boil, stirring to scrape up any brown bits from bottom. Stir in chicken stock and jelly; bring to boil. Dissolve cornstarch in 2 tbsp (25 mL) cold water and stir into skillet; cook, stirring, until thickened and smooth. Stir in any drippings from roasting pan; taste and adjust seasoning. Serve in heated sauceboat alongside platter of Cornish hens and pears. Garnish platter with watercress sprigs. Makes 4 servings.

The Wine

The sweetness of the pears, the red currant jelly and the port demand a certain amount of sweetness in the wine. You can either look for pearlike flavors (the Viognier grape and certain Chardonnays) or a natural sweetness (German Riesling Spätlese).

International option: Dry Vouvray (Loire) or Condrieu (Rhône).

Canadian option: B.C. Chenin Blanc or Bacchus.

Single white wine option: Riesling Spätlese Trocken (Rheingau).

Uncooked Cranberry Relish with Citrus and Fresh Ginger

1	each pink or red grapefruit and tangerine or orange	1
2 cups	cranberries	500 mL
1 tbsp	chopped fresh ginger	15 mL
1/2 cup	(approx) granulated sugar	125 mL
2 tbsp	fresh lime juice	25 mL

With zester or grater, remove zest from grapefruit and tangerine; set aside. Peel fruit and cut into segments, removing all pith, seeds and as much membrane as possible. In food processor, process segments until finely chopped; transfer to bowl.

Add cranberries and ginger to food processor; using on/off pulses, process just until chopped, being careful not to overprocess. Add to citrus fruit; stir in sugar, lime juice and reserved zest until sugar dissolves, adding more sugar if necessary. Cover and refrigerate for at least 30 minutes or for up to 2 weeks. Makes 2-1/2 cups (625 mL).

My favorite cooked cranberry sauce is just the simple recipe with sugar and water that appears on the package of cranberries. However, I do think an uncooked sauce is a nice change, and this one with a hint of ginger and lots of citrus is very refreshing. Try it with not only roast poultry but pâtés and meat pies as well.

Squash and Carrot Purée

Half	butternut squash (or 1 lb/500 g other winter squash)	Half
3	medium carrots, sliced (1/2 lb/250 g)	3
1 cup	water	250 mL
1-1/2 tsp	granulated sugar	7 mL
3 tbsp	butter	50 mL
1/2 tsp	salt	2 mL
Pinch	pepper	Pinch
1/4 cup	crème fraîche or sour cream	50 mL
2 tsp	minced fresh ginger	10 mL

Cut squash in half and remove seeds; place, cut side down, in shallow baking dish. Cover and bake in 350°F (180°C) oven for about 45 minutes or until quite tender.

Meanwhile, in saucepan, combine carrots, water, sugar, 1 tbsp (15 mL) of the butter, salt and pepper; bring to boil. Reduce heat to medium-low and cook, uncovered, until water evaporates and carrots are tender. (If water evaporates before carrots are done, add a bit more to pan.)

This smooth delicious purée, with a color to remind you of autumn leaves, makes a great do-ahead vegetable side dish.

Scrape squash from skin into food processor. Add carrots, crème fraîche, remaining butter and ginger; process, in batches if necessary, until smooth. Serve immediately. (Purée can be transferred to ovenproof dish; cooled, covered and refrigerated for up to 2 days. Reheat in microwave or in 350°F/180°C oven for 25 to 30 minutes.) Makes 4 servings.

Coconut Pumpkin Pie

A bit of shredded coconut gives the traditional Thanksgiving dessert a festive air. If possible, use unsweetened coconut.

	Pastry for 9-inch (23 cm) single-crust pie	
2	eggs	2
3/4 cup	packed brown sugar	175 mL
1-3/4 cups	puréed cooked pumpkin or	425 mL
	1 can (14 oz/398 mL) pumpkin	
1 tsp	ground cinnamon	5 mL
1/2 tsp	each ground ginger and allspice	2 mL
1/4 tsp	each ground cloves, nutmeg and salt	1 mL
1-1/3 cups	light cream	325 mL
3/4 cup	grated coconut	175 mL
1 tbsp	rum or brandy (optional)	15 mL
	Whipped cream	

On lightly floured surface, roll out pastry and line deep pie plate; refrigerate.

In large bowl, beat together eggs and sugar; beat in pumpkin, cinnamon, ginger, allspice, cloves, nutmeg and salt. Beat in cream. Stir in 1/2 cup (125 mL) of the coconut, and rum (if using).

Pour into pie shell; sprinkle with remaining coconut. Bake in 450°F (230°C) oven for 10 minutes. Reduce heat to 350°F (180°C); bake for about 45 minutes longer or until knife inserted in middle comes out clean, shielding pastry with foil if browning too quickly. Serve cool with whipped cream.

The Wine

The flavor of coconut can be found in wines that have been aged in new American oak. The spices in the pumpkin are quite dominant, so you will need a dessert wine with lots of character and sweetness but with balancing acidity. Moscatel de Setubal (Portugal) or any of the sweet Muscats from southern France (Beaumes de Venise, Rivesaltes) would be delicious.

A Late-Fall Supper for Eight

*Tiny Corn Pancakes
with Smoked Salmon and Crème Fraîche*

Onion and Stilton Soup

Pork Loin Roasted with Peppercorn and Herb Butter

Broccoli Purée

Brandied Squash Purée

Crisp Potato-Parmesan Cake

Basil-Pear Salad

Almond Plum Tart

Cinnamon Ice Cream

I love entertaining in the fall when the market is full of enticing fresh vegetables and fruits. With so many colorful, good things to choose from, menus just seem to design themselves.

This one is particularly appealing with its great array of tastes and textures. Except for cooking the pancakes, making gravy and putting together the last touches for the salad, the whole meal is make-ahead, too.

PARTY PRIMER

1. *Up to two days ahead, make Cinnamon Ice Cream.*
2. *Up to one day ahead, prepare batter for Corn Pancakes. Make Onion and Stilton Soup. Prepare pastry for Plum Tart.*
3. *Up to six hours ahead, make Broccoli and Squash Purées. Bake Almond Plum Tart.*
4. *Up to five hours ahead, prepare pork for roasting.*
5. *Up to four hours ahead, make and bake Potato-Parmesan Cake. Prepare dressing for Basil-Pear Salad.*
6. *Just before serving, reheat vegetable purées. Cook and complete Corn Pancakes. Add cream to soup and gently reheat. Make gravy for pork. Assemble salad.*
7. *Remove ice cream to refrigerator.*

Tiny Corn Pancakes with Smoked Salmon and Crème Fraîche

2	ears sweet corn (uncooked)	2
1 cup	light cream	250 mL
2	eggs	2
2 tbsp	butter, melted	25 mL
1/4 tsp	each salt and pepper	1 mL
1/2 cup	cornmeal	125 mL
1/2 cup	all-purpose flour	125 mL
	Vegetable oil	
3/4 cup	crème fraîche or good-quality sour cream	175 mL
1 tsp	fresh lemon juice	5 mL
4 oz	smoked salmon, cut in thin strips	125 g
	Fresh dill sprigs	
	Pickled baby corn (optional)	

These lovely little pancakes, which disappear in no time, are well worth the short last-minute preparation they require. Work quickly to make them in batches so that they stay 'warm,' but don't keep them 'hot' in an oven because the crème fraîche will melt.

Cut kernels from corn to make 1 cup (250 mL). Coarsely chop by hand or in food processor; set aside.

In blender, combine cream, eggs, butter, salt and pepper until smooth. Add cornmeal and flour; blend until smooth. Stir in corn kernels. (Recipe can be prepared to this point, covered and refrigerated for up to 1 day.)

Brush large nonstick griddle or skillet with oil; heat over medium-high heat. Pour about 1 tbsp (15 mL) batter for each pancake onto griddle; cook for about 2 minutes or until browned on bottom. Flip and cook for about 1 minute or until browned.

Stir together crème fraîche and lemon juice. Arrange pancakes in single layer on large warm serving platter. Top each pancake with

»

The Wine

The blandness of the corn pancakes and the crème fraîche sets off the smoky, salty taste of the smoked salmon heightened by the dill. Depending upon how elegant you want to be, you can match this delicious dish with a glass of Brut champagne. That would be my first choice, but the following wines would work well, too.

International option: Dry Alsatian Gewürztraminer or Chablis (Burgundy) or Pouilly-Fumé (Loire).

Canadian option: Ontario Aligoté or B.C. dry Riesling.

dollop of crème fraîche. Arrange strip of salmon over top; garnish with small sprig of dill. Garnish platter with bigger dill sprigs, and baby corn (if using). Makes about 3 dozen hors d'oeuvres.

ONION AND STILTON SOUP

Onions never tasted better than in this interesting, easy-to-make soup. Long, slow cooking makes them particularly sweet, a nice contrast to the tangy cheese.

Don't use all of the cheese mixture during the first serving. Everyone will want seconds!

2 tbsp	butter	25 mL
1 tbsp	vegetable oil	15 mL
2 lb	onions, thinly sliced	1 kg
2	cloves garlic, minced	2
8 cups	chicken stock	2 L
1-1/2 cups	dry white wine or dry vermouth	375 mL
1/4 tsp	each dried marjoram and thyme	1 mL
1-1/2 cups	light cream	375 mL
	Salt and pepper	
6 oz	Stilton cheese, crumbled	175 g
2 tbsp	chopped fresh parsley	25 mL

In large saucepan, melt butter with oil over medium-low heat; cook onions and garlic for 3 minutes, partially covered. Uncover and cook for 20 to 35 minutes or until onions are browned, stirring often. Add stock, wine, marjoram and thyme; bring to boil. Reduce heat and simmer, partially covered, for 30 minutes.

Remove 1-1/2 cups (375 mL) of the onions and set aside. Purée soup, in batches, in blender or food processor. Return to pan and add reserved onions. (Recipe can be prepared to this point, covered and refrigerated for up to 1 day.) Stir in cream, and salt and pepper to taste. Reheat gently, but do not boil. Transfer to heated soup tureen or warm soup bowls.

Meanwhile, stir together cheese and parsley; sprinkle about 1 tbsp (15 mL) on each serving. Makes 8 servings.

THE WINE

The creamy, tangy taste of this rich soup needs a contrasting flavor if you're serving wine (which I would in this case). To highlight the sharp cheese taste, I would select a sweet, well-chilled wine.

International option (all chilled): White port or Oloroso sherry or Pineau des Charentes.

Canadian option (both chilled): Cream sherry or Inniskillin Fleur d'Ontario.

Pork Loin Roasted with Peppercorn and Herb Butter

1/4 cup	unsalted butter, softened	50 mL
1/4 cup	chopped fresh parsley	50 mL
2 tbsp	assorted peppercorns, coarsely crushed	25 mL
1 tsp	dried basil	5 mL
1/2 tsp	salt	2 mL
1/4 tsp	each pepper and crushed dried rosemary	1 mL
2	cloves garlic, minced	2
1	boneless double loin pork roast (about 4 lb/2 kg)	1
1 cup	dry vermouth	250 mL
1 cup	vegetable or meat stock	250 mL
2 tbsp	cornstarch	25 mL
1/4 cup	cold water	50 mL
	Watercress or parsley	

A flavorful butter keeps this festive roast pork nice and juicy during roasting. A boneless loin is easiest to carve, but for a pretty presentation for carving at the table, you might use a 5 lb (2.2 kg) rack of pork — one from which the butcher removes the backbone but leaves the ribs.

In small bowl, cream butter; stir in parsley, peppercorns, basil, salt, pepper, rosemary and garlic.

Place roast, fat side up, on rack in shallow roasting pan. With sharp knife, cut pocket in middle on top of roast; make pocket at each end where loins meet. Stuff some butter mixture into each pocket; spread remainder on top of roast. (Roast can be prepared to this point and refrigerated for up to 4 hours. Remove from refrigerator 30 minutes before roasting.)

Place roast in 450°F (230°C) oven and immediately reduce heat to 325°F (160°C); roast for 1 hour. Add vermouth to pan and baste roast. Roast, basting occasionally, for 1 to 1-1/2 hours longer

≫

The Wine

Pork is a sweet meat given a more vital presence on the palate by the addition of the crushed peppercorns, garlic, basil and rosemary. For those who would rather drink white wine, this is a dish that can happily consort with red or white.

International option: Oregon Pinot Noir or red Burgundy or mature Rioja red (Spain).

Canadian option: Ontario or B.C. Pinot Noir.

White option: Full-bodied New World Chardonnay.

or until meat thermometer inserted in thickest part of roast reads 160°F (70°C). Remove roast to serving platter. Let stand for 15 minutes under loose tent of foil before slicing.

Remove excess fat from surface of pan drippings. Add stock and bring to boil, stirring to scrape up any brown bits from bottom of pan. Dissolve cornstarch in water; gradually stir into drippings and cook, stirring, until smooth and thickened.

Slice meat and serve garnished with watercress. Pass sauce separately in warmed sauceboat. Makes 8 servings.

Broccoli Purée

Broccoli makes a pretty and easy side dish when cooked and puréed ahead of time.

2	bunches broccoli	2
3	shallots, chopped	3
1/4 cup	sour cream	50 mL
2 tbsp	butter	25 mL
3/4 tsp	dried chervil	4 mL
	Salt and pepper	

Trim broccoli and cut into small florets; peel stems and chop. Place in saucepan along with shallots and cover with boiling salted water; bring to boil. Reduce heat and simmer, uncovered, for about 5 minutes or until tender. Drain well.

In food processor, purée broccoli mixture, sour cream, butter, chervil, and salt and pepper to taste until smooth. Transfer to ovenproof serving dish. (Purée can be cooled, covered and refrigerated for up to 6 hours; remove from refrigerator 30 minutes before reheating. Reheat, covered, in 350°F/180°C oven for 20 to 25 minutes or until heated through.) Makes 8 servings.

Brandied Squash Purée

1	large butternut squash (about 3-1/2 lb/1.75 kg)	1
1/2 cup	crème fraîche or sour cream	125 mL
2 tbsp	each butter and brandy	25 mL
1/4 tsp	ground ginger	1 mL
Pinch	ground nutmeg	Pinch
	Salt and pepper	

Cut squash in half and remove seeds; place, cut side down, in shallow glass baking dish. Cover with vented plastic wrap and microwave at High for about 10 minutes or until tender. Let stand for 5 minutes. (Alternatively, cover and bake in 350°F/180°C oven for 45 to 60 minutes or until tender.)

Scrape squash from skin into food processor. Add crème fraîche, butter, brandy, ginger, nutmeg, and salt and pepper to taste; purée until smooth. Transfer to ovenproof serving dish. (Recipe can be prepared to this point, cooled, covered and refrigerated for up to 6 hours; remove from refrigerator 30 minutes before reheating. Reheat, covered, in 350°F/180°C oven for 25 minutes or until heated through.) Makes 8 servings.

This is one of my favorite ways to serve one of my favorite vegetables. You can substitute another winter squash for the butternut, but be sure it's one that bakes to a smooth texture.

Crisp Potato-Parmesan Cake

8	large baking potatoes	8
1/3 cup	olive oil	75 mL
2	cloves garlic, minced	2
1/4 cup	coarsely chopped fresh rosemary (or 4 tsp/20 mL crushed dried)	50 mL
1 tsp	coarsely ground pepper	5 mL
1/2 tsp	each salt and paprika	2 mL
1-1/4 cups	freshly grated Parmesan cheese	300 mL

Peel potatoes and thinly slice. Brush inside of 10-inch (3 L) springform pan well with some of the oil. Toss potatoes with remaining oil, garlic, rosemary, pepper, salt and paprika.

Alternately layer potatoes and cheese in pan, making 4 layers of potatoes and 3 of cheese; set on baking sheet. Bake, uncovered, in 400°F (200°C) oven for about 1 hour or until top potatoes are brown and crispy. Let cool to room temperature before running knife around inside rim and transferring cake to platter. Cut into wedges to serve. Makes 8 servings.

Since this simple potato dish is served at room temperature, roast it before you put in the pork.

BASIL-PEAR SALAD

Most of the ingredients of pistou (French pesto) are found in the dressing for this refreshing, simple salad.

1/2 cup	olive oil	125 mL
1/4 cup	fresh lemon juice	50 mL
	Salt and pepper	
1/2 cup	slivered fresh basil leaves	125 mL
4	ripe Barlett pears	4
	Red leaf lettuce (about 1 small head)	
1/3 cup	toasted pine nuts	75 mL
1/3 cup	slivered Parmesan*	75 mL

In small bowl, whisk together oil, three-quarters of the lemon juice, and salt and pepper to taste; stir in basil. (Dressing can be covered and set aside for up to 4 hours.)

Core and thinly slice unpeeled pears; toss with remaining lemon juice.

Line salad plates with lettuce and arrange pear slices on top. Drizzle with dressing; sprinkle with pine nuts and Parmesan slivers. Sprinkle with freshly ground pepper and serve immediately. Makes 8 servings.

* To make slivers, run a vegetable parer across a short piece of Parmesan cheese.

Almond Plum Tart

Tart purple plums sit atop a smooth almond filling (frangipane) for an interesting combination of texture and color.

Sweet Short Pastry (Pâte Sucrée):

1-1/2 cups	all-purpose flour	375 mL
4 tsp	granulated sugar	20 mL
1/4 tsp	salt	1 mL
1/2 cup	chilled unsalted butter, cut in small bits	125 mL
2 tbsp	chilled shortening, cut in small bits	25 mL
1/4 cup	(approx) ice water	50 mL

Plum Frangipane Filling:

2/3 cup	ground blanched almonds	150 mL
2/3 cup	granulated sugar	150 mL
1	egg	1
2 tbsp	butter	25 mL
1 tsp	each vanilla and grated lemon zest	5 mL
1/4 tsp	almond extract	1 mL
15	prune plums, pitted and quartered	15
1/4 cup	currant jelly	50 mL
1 tbsp	port	15 mL

Sweet Short Pastry: In large bowl, stir together flour, sugar and salt. With fingertips, rub in butter and shortening until mixture resembles large oatmeal flakes. Do not let fat heat up.

Tossing mixture with cupped hand, sprinkle in water, 1 tbsp (15 mL) at a time and adding up to 1 tbsp (15 mL) more if necessary, until crumbs can be gathered into mass. Press firmly into ball. Place on lightly floured surface and smear about 2 tbsp (25 mL) at a time into 6-inch (15 cm) lengths across surface. Gather up dough and form into disc; dust with flour, wrap and chill for 1 hour or overnight.

On lightly floured surface, roll out as quickly as possible to about 3/16-inch (4 mm) thickness; roll around pin and lay over 9-inch (23 cm) flan pan. Unroll and fit pastry in pan. Chill for 15 minutes.

Line shell with foil; weigh down with dried beans or rice. Bake in 400°F (200°C) oven for 8 minutes. Remove beans and foil; prick bottom at 1/2 inch (1 cm) intervals and bake 2 to 3 minutes longer or until dry. Let cool completely.

Plum Frangipane Filling: In bowl, combine almonds, half of the sugar, egg, butter, vanilla, lemon zest and almond extract; spread over tart shell. Toss plums with remaining sugar; arrange over top. Bake in 350°F (180°C) oven for 40 minutes or until filling is set and pastry is browned. Cool on rack.

Heat currant jelly with port until melted and smooth. Spoon over tart; cool to room temperature.

CINNAMON ICE CREAM

There's just a hint of cinnamon in this ice cream that goes so well with fruit desserts.

1-1/2 cups	milk	375 mL
1 cup	whipping cream	250 mL
1	strip (2-inch/5 cm) lemon zest	1
1/2 tsp	ground cinnamon	2 mL
3	egg yolks	3
1/3 cup	granulated sugar	75 mL

In medium saucepan, heat milk, cream, lemon zest and cinnamon over medium heat until bubbles form around edge. Cool slightly.

In large bowl, whisk yolks and sugar until blended; gradually whisk in hot milk. Return to saucepan and cook over medium heat, stirring constantly, until mixture lightly coats back of spoon, about 5 minutes. Do not boil.

Strain through fine sieve into large clean bowl; cool, stirring occasionally. Cover and refrigerate for at least 2 hours or until chilled.

Transfer to ice-cream maker and freeze according to manufacturer's instructions. (Ice cream can be packed into container and frozen for up to 2 days; remove to refrigerator for 30 minutes before serving.) Makes about 4 cups (1 L).

THE WINE

The cinnamon flavor adds an interesting accent to the sweet-sour plum and currant jelly. The style of dessert wine requires good acidity yet lots of sweetness.

International option: German Riesling of Auslese or Beerenauslese quality or Gewürztraminer Vendange Tardive Selection de Grains Nobles (a long name for a great Alsatian dessert wine) or California Late Harvest Riesling.

Canadian option: Ontario or B.C. Icewine.

A Casual Dinner for Twelve

Fontina Gougère Ring with Prosciutto

Cornichons and Black Olives

Cod and Potato Cakes with Basil Oil

Braised Veal with Caramelized Vegetables

Crusty Bread

*Salad of Assorted Greens
with Fennel and Red Onion Vinaigrette*

Cheese and Fruit

Chocolate Hazelnut Torte

Buy or make lots of French sticks or crusty Italian bread for this meal. Everyone will want to use it to sop up every bit of the sauce from the veal and perhaps have a slice or two with the salad.

Then leave both the bread and butter on the table for the cheese course. Offer three or four different cheeses, surrounded by two or three types of grapes before the dessert. That way, the same bread and wine can do for both the main and cheese courses, and you can continue the meal with something savory before finishing off with the chocolate dessert and sweet dessert wine.

I make stews quite often for entertaining. They are better if made ahead and they're very easy to serve. For a dinner like this, I set a dinner plate for everyone, and top it with a smaller plate of Cod and Potato Cakes. After I remove that plate, I serve the stew in a shallow soup or pasta bowl that goes on the dinner plate, which in turn can hold the salad that I pass in a big bowl for guests to help themselves.

PARTY PRIMER

1. *Up to two days ahead, make Braised Veal with Caramelized Vegetables. Make Basil Oil. Wash and dry greens for salad.*
2. *Up to one day ahead, make Chocolate Hazelnut Torte.*
3. *Up to eight hours ahead, make Cod and Potato Cakes.*
4. *Several hours ahead, glaze torte.*
5. *Up to two hours ahead, make vinaigrette for salad; tear greens.*
6. *About one-and-a-half hours ahead, make Gougère Ring.*
7. *Reheat stew in oven, stirring often.*
8. *Fry cod cakes just before serving.*
9. *Toss salad just before serving.*

Fontina Gougère Ring with Prosciutto

7 or 8	eggs	7 or 8
1/2 tsp	salt	2 mL
1-1/2 cups	water	375 mL
1/3 cup	unsalted butter	75 mL
1 tsp	each Dijon mustard and granulated sugar	5 mL
1/2 tsp	dry mustard	2 mL
1/4 tsp	pepper	1 mL
Dash	hot pepper sauce	Dash
1-1/2 cups	all-purpose flour	375 mL
1-1/2 cups	shredded fontina cheese (about 6 oz/175 g)	375 mL
1 cup	chopped prosciutto	250 mL

With fork, beat together 1 of the eggs and pinch of the salt; set aside.

In medium saucepan, bring water, butter, Dijon mustard, sugar, dry mustard, pepper, hot pepper sauce and remaining salt to boil, stirring to melt butter. Remove from heat and immediately add flour all at once; beat with wooden spoon for 1 minute or until mixture is well combined and leaves sides of pan. Cook over medium heat for 2 minutes, stirring constantly.

Transfer mixture to food processor fitted with metal blade; cool for 1 to 2 minutes. Add 6 eggs and process, stopping once to scrape down side of bowl, until eggs are completely incorporated and mixture is very thick, smooth and shiny, about 30 seconds. Dough should be firm enough to hold its shape on edges of spoon but with slight slump at tip. If too thick, add remaining egg (or part of it) and process for 10 seconds.

Add three-quarters of the cheese; process for 5 seconds. With spoon, stir in prosciutto.

Grease two baking sheets and sprinkle with water, shaking off excess. Using finger, draw 9-inch (23 cm) circle on each. Using two large spoons, drop dough by spoonfuls onto circles so that rounds just touch to form ring. Brush with egg glaze, not letting it drip onto sheet. Sprinkle with remaining cheese. (Gougère can be covered with inverted bowl and set aside for up to 30 minutes.)

Place in 425°F (220°C) oven and immediately reduce temperature to 400°F (200°C); bake for 25 minutes. Reduce temperature to 375°F (190°C) and bake for another 20 minutes or until golden brown. Carefully remove to rack; cool for 5 minutes before placing on round serving plates. Cut into individual puffs to serve warm. Makes 12 servings.

This is one of my favorite appetizers to serve in the living room with drinks. It looks magnificent, but is actually very easy to make, especially using my food processor method. You can also make it with Gruyère cheese instead of fontina and skip the prosciutto if you wish. Insert dishes of black olives and cornichons in the middle of the rings.

THE WINE

The saltiness of the prosciutto is cut by the light cheese-flavored pastry allowing for a more fruity wine than the description of the gougère ring might suggest.

International option: Alsace Tokay-Pinot Gris or St. Véran from the Mâconnais (Southern Burgundy).

Canadian option: B.C. Pinot Blanc or Ontario Pinot Grigio.

Cod and Potato Cakes with Basil Oil

4 cups	water	1 L
1 cup	dry white wine	250 mL
1	bay leaf	1
1	sprig fresh thyme (or pinch dried)	1
2	cloves garlic	2
1-1/2 lb	fresh cod fillets	750 g
4	large potatoes, peeled and quartered	4
2 tbsp	butter	25 mL
1	onion, chopped	1
1/3 cup	milk	75 mL
1	egg, beaten	1
2 tsp	dried basil	10 mL
	Salt and pepper	
1/4 cup	all-purpose flour	50 mL
1/4 cup	(approx) olive oil	50 mL
	Basil Oil (recipe follows)	

When Jean-Georges Vongerichten, a young New York chef, guest-cooked at Ontario's Stratford Chefs School, I was lucky enough to meet him, get his mother's recipe for warm chocolate cake and taste some of his wonderful cod cakes. Like his, only in that they use fresh cod, these homey cakes are garnished with an adaptation of one of his famous flavored oils.

In large deep skillet, combine water, wine, bay leaf, thyme and 1 clove garlic; bring to simmer over medium-low heat. Add fish; cover and poach for 10 minutes. Remove fish and pat dry; flake with fork, removing any bones. Discard poaching liquid.

Meanwhile, in saucepan of boiling salted water, cook potatoes until tender, 20 to 25 minutes. Drain well and return to saucepan; heat for a few seconds to dry. Remove from heat; rice finely or mash well. Transfer to large bowl.

In skillet, melt butter over medium heat; cook onion, stirring, until softened, about 5 minutes. Add to potatoes along with cod, milk, egg, basil, and salt and pepper to taste. Form into 24 patties that are 2 inches (5 cm) wide and 1 inch (2.5 cm) thick. Dredge in flour, gently shaking off excess. (Cakes can be prepared to this

》》

point, placed on rack on baking sheet, covered and refrigerated for up to 8 hours.)

In two large skillets, heat 1 to 2 tbsp (15 to 25 mL) oil over medium-high heat; fry cakes until golden brown on both sides, about 6 minutes, turning once and adding more oil if necessary. Drizzle Basil Oil around edge of 12 warm salad plates; place two cakes in middle of each. Serve immediately. Makes 12 servings.

Basil Oil:

1/3 cup	each olive oil and basil leaves	75 mL
	Salt and pepper	

In blender, blend half of the oil with the basil. Season with salt and pepper to taste. Combine in jar with remaining oil; let stand for 24 hours. Push through fine sieve, pressing to get as much basil color as possible. Discard basil. Oil can be kept at room temperature for up to 2 days.

THE WINE

Cod and garlic combined with the fried taste require a hefty white wine with good acidity, especially if you are following the Tokay-Pinot Gris.

International option: White Rhône or Spanish or Portuguese white.

Canadian option: Chardonnay (not barrel-fermented or barrel-aged).

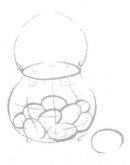

Braised Veal
with Caramelized Vegetables

6 lb	boneless veal, cut in 1-inch (2.5 cm) cubes	2.7 kg
3/4 cup	all-purpose flour	175 mL
1/2 cup	(approx) olive oil	125 mL
1 tsp	paprika	5 mL
1/3 cup	minced shallots	75 mL
2 cups	dry vermouth	500 mL
2-1/2 cups	chicken stock	625 mL
2 tsp	crumbled dried sage	10 mL
1/2 tsp	each crumbled dried rosemary and thyme	2 mL
	Salt and pepper	
1/4 cup	butter	50 mL
2 tbsp	brown sugar	25 mL
2	pkg (each 10 oz/283 g) pearl onions, peeled	2
1-1/2 lb	mini carrots	750 g
6	small turnips, peeled and cut in wedges	6
4	parsnips, cut in 1-inch (2.5 cm) pieces	4
	Sprigs fresh rosemary, sage or thyme	

Tender chunks of veal and vegetables kept crisp by doing them separately combine in a velvety sauce.

Dry veal and dredge lightly with flour. In large heavy casserole or Dutch oven, heat half the oil over medium-high heat; cook veal, in batches and adding oil only if necessary, until browned on all sides. Remove with slotted spoon to plate; sprinkle with paprika.

In casserole, heat more oil if necessary; cook shallots for 3 minutes over medium heat. Stir in vermouth and 1-1/2 cups (375 mL) of the stock; bring to boil, scraping up brown bits in bottom of pan.

Return veal and any juices to pot; add sage, rosemary, thyme, and salt and pepper to taste. Cover, reduce heat and simmer for about 1-1/4 hours or until veal is tender, stirring occasionally.

Meanwhile, in deep skillet or shallow stovetop casserole, melt butter and sugar; add onions, carrots, turnips and parsnips, stirring to coat. Sprinkle with salt and pepper to taste; add remaining stock and bring to boil.

Bake, uncovered and stirring occasionally, in 350°F (180°C) oven for 45 minutes or until vegetables are tender. Stir into cooked veal. (Stew can be cooled, covered and refrigerated for up to 2 days; reheat slowly on stovetop, stirring often, or place in 350°F/180°C oven, covered, for about 30 minutes or until heated through.) Serve in heated shallow soup or pasta bowls garnished with sprig of fresh herb. Makes 12 servings.

Veal is a very forgiving meat. Its gentle flavor allows you to pair it with either white or red wine that's not too aggressive. Since there is some sweetness in the vegetables, go for a wine with good, up-front fruit.

International option: Oregon Pinot Noir or Chilean Merlot.

Canadian option: Ontario Cabernet Franc.

White wine throughout the meal option: White Burgundy or Ontario barrel-aged Chardonnay.

SALAD OF ASSORTED GREENS WITH FENNEL AND RED ONION VINAIGRETTE

A simple green salad gets extra flavor and crunch from a vinaigrette of fennel and red onion and a sprinkle of toasted pine nuts.

1	small fennel bulb	1
2/3 cup	minced red onion	150 mL
1/2 cup	olive oil	125 mL
2 tbsp	each balsamic and white wine vinegar	25 mL
2	cloves garlic, minced	2
1	head romaine lettuce	1
2	heads radicchio	2
2	heads Belgian endive	2
	Salt and pepper	
1/2 cup	toasted pine nuts	125 mL

Trim fennel and chop finely. Combine with red onion, oil, balsamic and white wine vinegar and garlic. (Vinaigrette can be set aside for up to 2 hours.)

Tear romaine lettuce, radicchio and endive into bite-sized pieces. Place in salad bowl and toss with salt and pepper to taste. (Greens can be covered with damp tea towel and refrigerated for up to 2 hours).

To serve, toss greens with vinaigrette. Sprinkle with pine nuts. Makes 12 servings.

Chocolate Hazelnut Torte

1/4 cup	chopped dried apricots	50 mL
1/4 cup	Frangelico liqueur or rum	50 mL
6 oz	bittersweet chocolate, coarsely chopped	175 g
1/2 cup	unsalted butter, cut in pieces	125 mL
3	eggs, separated	3
2/3 cup	granulated sugar	150 mL
1/4 cup	all-purpose flour	50 mL
2/3 cup	ground hazelnuts (filberts)	150 mL
Pinch	cream of tartar	Pinch
Glaze:		
1/3 cup	whipping cream	75 mL
6 oz	semisweet chocolate, chopped	175 g

I have several friends who are 'chocoholics,' including (as I discovered when I served him this cake) my co-author. You don't have to be addicted, however, to enjoy this dense torte with its liqueur-soaked apricots. The simplicity of the dessert is well concealed by its wonderful appearance and taste, too.

Combine apricots and Frangelico; set aside.

In top of double boiler, melt chocolate and butter over simmering water, stirring until smooth. Remove from heat and cool slightly.

In large bowl, beat egg yolks with 1/2 cup (125 mL) of the sugar until pale and thickened. Stir in chocolate mixture, flour and ground hazelnuts. Stir in apricot mixture.

In another large bowl with clean beaters, beat egg whites until foamy. Add cream of tartar and beat at medium speed until soft peaks form. Gradually add remaining sugar and beat until stiff but not dry peaks form; fold about one-quarter into chocolate mixture. Fold in remaining whites until just mixed.

Scrape batter into well-greased and floured 9-inch (2.5 L) springform pan, tapping on counter to level top. Bake in 375°F (190°C) oven until edge is dry but centre is still moist, about 30 minutes. Do not overbake. Let cool completely on rack before removing pan. (Torte can be made to this point, covered, and set aside for up to 1 day.)

Glaze: In small saucepan, bring cream to boil over medium-low heat; add chocolate and stir until melted and smooth. Let cool until spreadable.

Place strips of waxed paper under edge of cake; spread cake with glaze. (Cake can be glazed several hours ahead and left in cool place.) Makes 12 small servings.

THE WINE

A very rich dessert where the flavors of the apricots meld beautifully with the chocolate. (I had two helpings!) An orange-flavored wine such as Quady's Essencia (California) is a perfect match.

An Updated Traditional Christmas Dinner for Eight

*Mushroom Salad
with Tangerine and Roasted Walnuts*

Herbed Roast Capon with Date-Pistachio Stuffing

Cranberry-Port Sauce

Creamy Whipped Potatoes

Sage Green Beans with Parmesan Slivers

Caramelized Rutabaga

Frozen Mincemeat Meringue Torte

Roast poultry, cranberry sauce, rutabaga, mince-meat — the traditional foods of a Canadian Christmas that everyone looks forward to seeing on the holiday table. Here, the dishes appear with little modern twists to make them so appealing they're bound to become new family traditions at your house.

PARTY PRIMER

1. *Up to three weeks ahead, make and freeze Mincemeat Meringue Torte.*
2. *Up to one week ahead, prepare Cranberry-Port Sauce.*
3. *One day ahead, marinate mushrooms for Salad. Make Date Pistachio Stuffing.*
4. *Up to eight hours ahead, pre-cook green beans.*
5. *Up to six hours ahead, cook Caramelized Rutabaga.*
6. *Prepare and roast capon.*
7. *Thirty minutes before serving, finish dressing for salad; then arrange salad just before serving.*
8. *Cook and mash potatoes. Add cream and reheat rutabaga. Reheat and finish Sage Green Beans. Remove torte to refrigerator.*
9. *Make sauce for capon.*

Mushroom Salad with Tangerine and Roasted Walnuts

1/3 cup	olive oil	75 mL
2 tbsp	tangerine or fresh orange juice	25 mL
2 tbsp	white wine vinegar	25 mL
1 tbsp	coarsely grated tangerine or orange zest	15 mL
1	clove garlic, minced	1
1 lb	small white mushrooms	500 g
1 cup	crème fraîche	250 mL
2 tbsp	snipped chives or green onion tops	25 mL
	Salt and pepper	
2	heads Belgian endive, separated	2
1	head radicchio, separated	1
1/2 cup	toasted coarsely chopped walnuts	125 mL

Most of this colorful and refreshing first course salad can be prepared a day ahead. If you can't find really tiny mushrooms, quarter larger ones.

In glass bowl, whisk together oil, tangerine juice, vinegar, tangerine zest and garlic; add mushrooms and toss to coat. Cover and refrigerate for up to 24 hours.

Half an hour before serving, fold in crème fraîche, chives, and salt and pepper to taste. Cover and refrigerate.

To serve, arrange 4 endive leaves like spokes of wheel around each edge of 8 salad plates; place radicchio leaves between endive leaves. Mound mushroom mixture in centre; sprinkle with toasted walnuts. Makes 8 servings.

The Wine

If there is one gustatory event in the year when no expense is spared, it has to be Christmas dinner. It's the meal when extra leaves are put in the dining-room table (or the fold-away card table is added to it) in order to accommodate visiting family and friends. Since there are usually lots of people sitting down to the meal, you can offer a selection of wines.

The salad's refreshing tangerine taste softened by the cream and the fleshy texture of the mushrooms suggest a medium-bodied white wine with good acidity.

International option: A Pinot Blanc from Alsace or a German Sylvaner.

Canadian option: Ontario dry Vidal; B.C. Chenin Blanc

Herbed Roast Capon with Date-Pistachio Stuffing

Capons, roosters desexed when young, grow big and fat and are therefore delicate and tender with lots of white meat and mild flavor. They are worth seeking out at farmers' markets and delicatessens. If you can't find one, substitute a small turkey, which will require a bit longer to cook.

8 lb	capon	3.5 kg
Half	lemon	Half
	Salt and pepper	
	Date-Pistachio Stuffing (recipe page 146)	
2 tbsp	each melted butter and Dijon mustard	25 mL
1 tsp	paprika	5 mL
2	cloves garlic, minced	2
1/2 tsp	each crumbled dried sage and marjoram	2 mL
1 cup	dry white wine or chicken stock	250 mL
1 tbsp	cornstarch	15 mL

Remove neck and giblets from capon; pat dry inside and out. Rub with lemon half inside and out, squeezing juice onto capon as you work. Sprinkle with salt and pepper inside and out.

Stuff cavities with Date-Pistachio Stuffing; truss bird. (Place any extra stuffing in casserole; cover and refrigerate until baking for last hour of capon's roasting, sprinkling once or twice with pan drippings.) In small bowl, stir together butter, mustard, paprika, garlic, sage and marjoram; spread all over capon.

Place capon on its side on rack in shallow roasting pan. Roast in 325°F (160°C) oven for 1 hour. Using oven mitts protected with foil, turn onto other side and roast for 1 hour longer.

Turn onto back and roast for 30 to 60 minutes longer or until juices run clear when thigh is pierced and meat thermometer registers 185°F (85°C) in thigh.

Transfer capon to cutting board and cover loosely with foil; let stand for 15 minutes before carving.

Discard any fat from drippings in pan. Add wine and bring to boil, stirring to scrape up any brown bits from bottom. Dissolve cornstarch in 2 tbsp (25 mL) cold water; stir into pan and cook, stirring, until smooth and thickened. Pass in warm sauceboat with capon. Makes 8 servings.

Date-Pistachio Stuffing:

1-1/2 cups	chopped pitted dates	375 mL
1 cup	hot chicken stock	250 mL
2 tbsp	butter	25 mL
2	onions, chopped	2
1 cup	chopped celery	250 mL
6 cups	cubed slightly stale bread	1.5 L
1 cup	shelled unsalted pistachio nuts	250 mL
1/4 cup	chopped fresh parsley	50 mL
1/2 tsp	each crumbled dried sage, marjoram and salt	2 mL
1/4 tsp	pepper	1 mL

Soak dates in stock for 30 minutes. In large skillet, melt butter over medium heat; cook onions and celery for 5 minutes, stirring often. Remove from heat; stir in bread, nuts, parsley, sage, marjoram, salt, pepper and date mixture. Let cool. (Stuffing can be covered and refrigerated for up to 1 day; let stand at room temperature for 30 minutes before stuffing capon.) Makes 6 cups (1.5 L).

The Wine

The date-pistachio stuffing adds a sweetness to the bird for which you will have to compensate with a medium-weight red wine with good fruit extract. The sauce also adds sweetness to the dish. That suggests a Pinot Noir from a warm growing area such as California.

International option: California Pinot Noir, Oregon Pinot Noir, Australian Cabernet/Shiraz.

Canadian option: Ontario Cabernet Franc.

White wine option: Alsace Pinot Blanc.

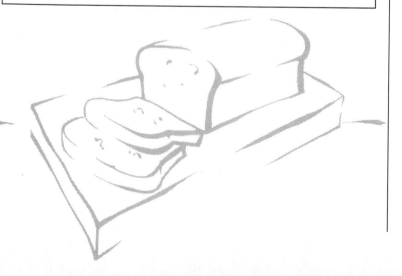

CRANBERRY-PORT SAUCE

This flavorful sauce is just right to serve with the Roast Capon or any other roast poultry. In a pretty jar, it also makes an inviting hostess gift.

1-1/2 cups	Port (ruby)	375 mL
1-1/2 cups	granulated sugar	375 mL
2 tsp	grated lemon zest	10 mL
Pinch	ground cloves	Pinch
1 lb	cranberries (4 cups/1 L)	500 g

In heavy saucepan, combine Port, sugar, lemon zest and cloves; bring to boil, stirring until sugar is dissolved. Add cranberries and bring to boil; boil, stirring constantly, for 5 to 8 minutes or until skins pop. Cool, cover and refrigerate for up to 1 week. Makes 3 cups (750 mL).

SAGE GREEN BEANS
WITH PARMESAN SLIVERS

The beans for this delightful side dish can be cooked ahead of time. They take only minutes to reheat, season and garnish. To make Parmesan slivers, run a vegetable parer across a short piece of Parmesan cheese.

2 lb	green beans, trimmed	1 kg
2	cloves garlic, each halved	2
3 tbsp	olive oil	50 mL
1 tsp	crumbled dried sage	5 mL
	Salt and pepper	
2 tsp	fresh lemon juice	10 mL
1/2 cup	slivered Parmesan cheese	125 mL

In large saucepan, bring large quantity of salted water to boil; cook beans over medium-high heat, uncovered, for about 5 minutes or until tender but firm. Drain and refresh under cold running water. (Beans can be prepared to this point, wrapped in clean tea towel and refrigerated for up to 8 hours.)

In large skillet, brown garlic in oil over medium heat. Discard garlic. Add beans and shake pan to coat. Season with sage, and salt and pepper to taste. Cover and cook over low heat for about 2 minutes or until heated through. Toss with lemon juice and arrange in shallow serving dish. Sprinkle with Parmesan slivers. Makes 8 servings.

CARAMELIZED RUTABAGA

3 lb	rutabaga (1 large)	1.5 kg
2 tbsp	butter	25 mL
2 tbsp	granulated sugar	25 mL
3/4 cup	chicken stock	175 mL
5	cloves garlic, thinly sliced	5
Pinch	each ground nutmeg and dried thyme	Pinch
	Salt and pepper	
1/4 cup	whipping cream	50 mL
2 tbsp	chopped chives or fresh parsley	25 mL

Peel and cut rutabaga into 1-inch (2.5 cm) cubes. In large pot of boiling water, cook rutabaga until just tender, about 12 minutes. Drain well.

In large skillet, melt butter over medium heat; cook rutabaga and sugar, stirring often, for 10 minutes. Reduce heat and add stock and garlic; cover and cook for 20 minutes.

Uncover and boil any remaining liquid for 1 minute or until most of the liquid evaporates. Stir in nutmeg, thyme, and salt and pepper to taste. (Rutabaga can be prepared to this point, covered and refrigerated for up to 6 hours. Reheat gently before proceeding.)

Stir in cream and warm through, stirring often. Taste and adjust seasoning. Sprinkle with chives to serve. Makes 8 servings.

Everyone looks for rutabaga on the Christmas dinner table, and this updated version is a joy to make because it can be almost entirely prepared ahead.

FROZEN MINCEMEAT MERINGUE TORTE

2/3 cup	egg whites (about 5)	150 mL
Pinch	each cream of tartar and salt	Pinch
1 cup	granulated sugar	250 mL
2 cups	vanilla ice cream	500 mL
1/2 cup	good-quality mincemeat	125 mL
2 cups	whipping cream	500 mL
2 tbsp	each icing sugar and dark rum	25 mL
8	walnut or pecan halves	8

Cover two baking sheets with parchment or brown paper. Lightly draw 10-inch (25 cm) circle on each.

In large bowl, beat egg whites until foamy; beat in cream of tartar and salt until soft peaks form. Gradually beat in sugar over 10-second period and continue to beat for 10 seconds. Spoon onto baking sheets, spreading to fill circles and smoothing tops with spatula.

Bake in 200°F (95°C) oven for 4 hours. Turn off oven and

Old-fashioned mincemeat is used in a whole new way in this easy dessert, the components of which can be made in stages. The whole torte can be made weeks ahead and frozen.

leave meringues inside to dry until cool, at least 6 hours or overnight. Gently peel off paper.

Let ice cream soften just enough to scoop into big bowl. Fold in mincemeat; place in freezer.

In large bowl, beat whipping cream, icing sugar and rum until stiff. Cover and refrigerate.

Place I meringue layer, flat side down, on large serving plate. Spread ice cream evenly over top to edge. Spread with slightly less than half the whipped cream. Top with second meringue layer, flat side up. Coat top and sides with remaining cream, working quickly so ice cream doesn't melt. Garnish top edge with nut halves.

Freeze torte until solid, at least 4 hours. Cover loosely with plastic wrap; overwrap torte and plate with foil to completely enclose. Freeze for up to 3 weeks. Place in refrigerator 30 minutes before serving. Makes 8 to I2 servings.

THE WINE

A very sweet dish like this torte cries out for a very sweet wine, nicely chilled. Or you could accompany it with a sweet sparkling wine such as Asti Spumante.

International option: Marsala dolce (sweet), Samos Muscat (Greece) or Cream Sherry.

Canadian option: Cream Sherry (well chilled).

An Elegant New Year's Eve Midnight Supper for Eight

Cognac Pear Pâté and Toasts

Cornichons

Smoked Salmon Spirals

Smoked Goose and Pears with Cranberry Horseradish Cream

Lamb Racks Provençal

Gratin Dauphinois

Sage-Glazed Carrots

Coffee Pavlova with Walnut Chantilly Cream

Chocolate Praline Truffle Squares

This menu should see you right through from early evening when you set out the pâté, through passing the smoked salmon appetizers in the living room, past the first sit-down course of Smoked Goose, until well after the midnight supper when you send guests off into the early morning with the memory of the crunchy-smooth chocolate truffle squares still vivid.

I often serve cornichons with pâté or other appetizers and obviously make them in the summer when tiny cucumbers are in season.

PARTY PRIMER

1. *Make Cornichons when cucumbers are in season.*
2. *Months ahead or up to two weeks ahead, make and freeze or refrigerate Chocolate Praline Truffle Squares.*
3. *Up to four days ahead, prepare Gratin Dauphinois.*
4. *Up to three days ahead, make Cognac Pear Pâté.*
5. *Up to two days ahead, make Cranberry Horseradish Cream. Make meringue for pavlova.*
6. *Up to one day ahead, make smoked salmon roll.*
7. *Up to four hours ahead, marinate Lamb Racks.*
8. *One hour before serving, remove lamb from refrigerator.*
9. *Just before serving, slice smoked salmon roll and arrange on cucumber slices.*
10. *Reheat Gratin Dauphinois. Cook carrots.*
11. *Just before serving, finish smoked goose plates.*
12. *Just before serving, finish pavlova.*

COGNAC PEAR PÂTÉ

1 cup	unsalted butter	250 mL
1 lb	chicken livers, rinsed	500 g
1	onion, sliced	1
2	small pears (or 1 large), peeled and thinly sliced	2
1/4 cup	cognac or brandy	50 mL
1/4 cup	whipping cream	50 mL
1 tsp	each dry mustard and salt	5 mL
1/4 tsp	each ground nutmeg, ground cloves, dried thyme and pepper	1 mL
Pinch	cayenne pepper	Pinch

This easy chicken liver pâté is creamy and mellow with the addition of a pear. Serve with crisp crackers, bread or toast.

In large skillet, melt 1/4 cup (50 mL) of the butter over medium heat; cook livers, stirring, for about 4 minutes or until browned all over yet still pink in centre. Remove with slotted spoon to food processor.

Add onion to pan and cook over medium heat, stirring often, for 5 minutes or until softened. Stir in pears and cook for 4 minutes. Add to chicken livers.

Add cognac to pan and bring to boil, stirring to scrape up any brown bits from pan; add to livers. Add cream, mustard, salt, nutmeg, cloves, thyme, pepper and cayenne; process until smooth. With motor running, add remaining butter, in pieces; process until very smooth. Pour into crock; cover and refrigerate at least overnight and for up to 3 days. Makes 3 cups (750 mL).

CORNICHONS

16 cups	small pickling cucumbers (gherkin size)	4 L
1-3/4 cups	pickling salt	425 mL
2 tbsp	white vinegar	25 mL
3/4 lb	small pickling onions	375 g
16	cloves garlic	16
8	sprigs each fresh thyme and tarragon	8
8	bay leaves	8
4 tsp	black and white peppercorns	20 mL
4 tsp	whole cloves	20 mL
8	dried hot chili peppers	8
6 cups	white wine vinegar	1.5 L

If I don't take time to make any other pickles during the summer, I do still make a batch of these little sour gherkins. I buy the smallest pickling cucumbers I can find that are really fresh looking. Then my husband helps me by scrubbing and drying each little cucumber (the most time-consuming task in making these easy uncooked pickles).

Wash cucumbers well; rub with towel to remove spikes. Place in stainless steel or glass bowl; sprinkle with salt and let stand overnight.

Rinse eight 2-cup (500 mL) preserving jars with boiling water; turn upside down to drain.

Drain cucumbers; cover with cold water and add the white vinegar. Drain again and pat dry. Evenly divide among jars along with onions, garlic, thyme, tarragon, bay leaves, peppercorns, cloves and chili peppers. Cover with vinegar. Seal jars and refrigerate for 5 weeks before using. Cornichons can be refrigerated for up to 1 year. Makes 16 cups (4 L).

SMOKED SALMON SPIRALS

These pretty little mouthfuls make a small amount of smoked salmon go a long way and are just right for a fancy party. Be sure to use regular cream cheese (not light or whipped), so that it hardens enough to slice.

1	pkg (250 g) cream cheese, softened	1
1 tsp	grated lemon zest	5 mL
2 tbsp	fresh lemon juice	25 mL
2 tbsp	rinsed drained capers	25 mL
2 tbsp	snipped fresh dill	25 mL
1 tbsp	Dijon mustard	15 mL
1/2 tsp	pepper	2 mL
1/2 lb	thinly sliced smoked salmon	250 g
1	English cucumber	1

In small bowl, combine cream cheese, lemon zest, lemon juice, capers, dill, mustard and pepper.

On large sheet of waxed paper, spread out salmon slices, slightly overlapping, to form rectangle. Roll thicker slices with rolling pin to thin slightly. Spread carefully with cream cheese mixture. Using paper as guide, roll up salmon tightly from one long side, jelly roll-style. Wrap tightly in plastic wrap; refrigerate for at least 2 hours, or until firm or for up to 24 hours.

Just before serving, with sharp knife, carefully cut into 1/3-inch (8 mm) thick slices. Slice cucumber; top each slice with salmon spiral. Arrange on platter and serve at once. Makes about 3 dozen.

THE WINE

The operative word here is *elegant*. To start the New Year off on the right note, champagne is the order of the day with the appetizers. And eight is the perfect number for a bottle, allowing a glass each.

Brut Champagne (or if you really want to put on the dog, a still white wine from the Champagne region, Coteaux champenoise – which isn't that easy to find).

SMOKED GOOSE AND PEARS WITH CRANBERRY HORSERADISH CREAM

1/2 lb	smoked goose breast	250 g
2	large pears	2
1/4 cup	fresh lemon juice	50 mL
1	bunch watercress	1
Cranberry Horseradish Cream:		
2 cups	cranberries	500 mL
1/2 cup	water	125 mL
1/3 cup	granulated sugar	75 mL
1/2 cup	sour cream	125 mL
1 tsp	horseradish	5 mL

Markets and delis often carry smoked goose around holiday time. If you can't find it in your area, substitute smoked duck or smoked turkey in this simple and pretty first course. If you use smoked duck, buy a little extra to make up for the fat that will need to be trimmed from the breasts.

Cranberry Horseradish Cream: In small saucepan, bring cranberries, water and sugar to boil over medium-high heat; boil, stirring often, for 5 minutes or until cranberries have popped and are soft.

In food processor or blender, purée cranberry mixture; push through fine sieve into small bowl. Stir in sour cream and horseradish. (Sauce can be covered and refrigerated for up to 2 days.)

Just before serving, cut goose on the diagonal into thin slices; arrange on 8 salad plates. Peel, core and thinly slice pears, sprinkling with lemon juice as you work; arrange on plates. Garnish with watercress. Serve with Cranberry Horseradish Cream. Makes 8 servings.

THE WINE

Goose has a rich flavor, especially when smoked. The acidity of the pears and cranberries contrast nicely and the bite of the horseradish adds another taste sensation. The wine has to envelop and heighten all of these tastes.

International option: Pouilly-Fumé from the Loire, New Zealand Sauvignon Blanc or Tokay-Pinot Gris from Alsace.

Canadian option: B.C. Pinot Blanc or Ontario barrel-fermented Chardonnay.

Lamb Racks Provençal

Seek out oven-ready lamb racks or have your butcher 'French' the ends of the bones for this easy and flavorful treatment of a very elegant cut of meat. However, you can easily French the racks yourself by scraping the rib bones clean of meat, fat and gristle to about 1 inch (2.5 cm) down from tips.

4	lamb racks (7 to 8 ribs each)	4
5	cloves garlic	5
1/2 cup	loosely packed parsley sprigs	125 mL
2 tbsp	olive oil	25 mL
2 tbsp	anchovy paste	25 mL
1 tbsp	red wine vinegar	15 mL
2 tsp	crushed dried rosemary	10 mL
1 tsp	coarsely ground pepper	5 mL
1/2 tsp	dried thyme	2 mL

Dry lamb racks well and score outside layer of fat diagonally to make small diamonds. In blender or food processor, process garlic, parsley, oil, anchovy paste, vinegar, rosemary, pepper and thyme until smooth. Rub all over racks. Marinate, covered, in refrigerator for up to 4 hours. Remove from refrigerator 30 minutes before roasting.

Place, bone side down, in shallow roasting pan. Roast in 450°F (230°C) oven for 10 minutes. Lower temperature to 350°F (180°C); roast for 20 to 30 minutes longer or until thermometer registers 140°F (60°C). Let stand, loosely covered with foil, for 10 minutes before carving between ribs to serve. Makes 8 servings.

The Wine

The lamb's rosemary and thyme work very well with the Cabernet Sauvignon grape.

International option: Château-bottled Bordeaux, Washington, Californian or Australian Cabernet Sauvignon.

Canadian option: Ontario Cabernet Sauvignon or Cabernet Franc.

Single wine option: Champagne Brut throughout the meal.

GRATIN DAUPHINOIS

2-1/2 lb	baking potatoes (about 8)	1.25 kg
2-3/4 cups	milk	675 mL
2 cups	whipping cream	500 mL
	Salt, white pepper and freshly grated nutmeg	
1	clove garlic, halved	1
1/2 cup	shredded Gruyère or Swiss cheese	125 mL

Peel potatoes. Cut into 1/8-inch (3 mm) thick slices, dropping into milk in large saucepan as you work. Bring to boil; reduce heat to medium-low and simmer, uncovered, for 10 minutes, being careful milk does not scorch. Drain, reserving milk for a soup or sauce.

Return potatoes to pan along with cream. Season to taste with salt, pepper and nutmeg. Bring to boil; reduce heat to low, cover and simmer until potatoes are very tender, about 15 minutes, watching again that mixture doesn't scorch.

Meanwhile, rub garlic over shallow 8-cup (2 L) baking dish; butter well. Mince garlic and sprinkle into dish; top with potato mixture. Sprinkle with cheese. (Recipe can be cooled, covered and refrigerated for up to 4 days.)

Bake, uncovered, in 350°F (180°C) oven for 25 to 30 minutes or until very hot and golden brown on top. Makes 8 servings.

Very rich, but truly glorious, this is the French version of scalloped potatoes. The potatoes are first simmered in milk to remove their acidity, then in cream for a make-ahead dish that's perfect for company.

SAGE-GLAZED CARROTS

2 lb	fresh mini carrots	1 kg
2 tbsp	butter	25 mL
	Salt and pepper	
1 cup	chicken stock	250 mL
1 tbsp	granulated sugar	15 mL
1 tsp	crushed dried sage	5 mL

Leave carrot tops and tails on; scrub well. In large skillet, melt butter over medium heat; cook carrots and salt and pepper to taste for 1 minute, stirring. (Carrots can be prepared to this point and set aside for up to 2 hours.) Add stock, sugar and sage; cook, uncovered, for 5 to 7 minutes or until carrots are tender-crisp and stock has evaporated. Makes 8 servings.

Neil Baxter, chef of Rundles Restaurant in Stratford, Ontario, runs cooking-class weekends that I attend every spring. When I failed miserably at 'turning' carrots, I suggested to Neil that we go to the grocery store nearby to buy mini carrots that are already 'turned' by nature.

Coffee Pavlova
with Walnut Chantilly Cream

A dessert originating in Australia, where it is usually topped with kiwifruit or passion fruit, Pavlova provides a light, satisfying close to a big meal.

2 tsp	instant coffee granules	10 mL
8	egg whites (1 cup/250 mL)	8
1-1/2 cups	granulated sugar	375 mL
4 tsp	white vinegar	20 mL
4 tsp	cornstarch	20 mL
1 tsp	vanilla	5 mL

Walnut Chantilly Cream:

1/3 cup	coarsely chopped walnuts	75 mL
2 tbsp	milk	25 mL
1 tsp	granulated sugar	5 mL
1 tsp	instant coffee granules	5 mL
2 cups	whipping cream	500 mL
2 tbsp	icing sugar	25 mL
1 tbsp	brandy or cognac	15 mL
	Fresh fruit or chocolate-covered coffee beans	

In small bowl, dissolve instant coffee granules in 2 tsp (10 mL) boiling water. Set aside to cool.

In large bowl, beat egg whites until soft peaks form. Very gradually add sugar, beating until stiff shiny peaks form. Stir vinegar, cornstarch and vanilla into coffee mixture until cornstarch dissolves; fold into egg whites. Carefully spread into greased 11- to 12-inch (28 to 30 cm) round baking dish, building up sides to form well in middle. Or, line large baking sheet with parchment paper; lightly draw 11-inch (28 cm) circle on paper. Spread meringue over circle, building up sides to make well in centre.

Bake in 300°F (150°C) oven for 30 minutes. Reduce heat to 200°F (100°C) and bake for 1-1/2 hours longer. Turn off oven and leave meringue inside to dry until cool, at least 2 hours. (Meringue can be stored in airtight container for up to 2 days.)

Walnut Chantilly Cream: In small saucepan, bring walnuts, milk, granulated sugar and coffee granules to boil; boil, uncovered, for 2 minutes or until liquid evaporates, watching carefully. Let cool.

Just before serving, whip cream with icing sugar. Fill pastry bag fitted with large star tip with some of the whipped cream. Fold brandy and boiled walnuts into remaining cream; pile into well in meringue. Pipe rosettes around edge. Garnish with fruit. (Or, add brandy and walnuts to all the cream and swirl it into meringue with spoon.) Makes 8 servings.

CHOCOLATE PRALINE TRUFFLE SQUARES

1/2 cup	whole hazelnuts	125 mL
1/2 cup	granulated sugar	125 mL
3 tbsp	water	50 mL
1/2 cup	whipping cream	125 mL
12 oz	dark bittersweet chocolate, chopped	375 g
3 tbsp	Frangelico liqueur	50 mL
	Unsweetened cocoa powder	

Toast hazelnuts on baking sheet in 350°F (180°C) oven for about 5 minutes or until fragrant. Rub in clean tea towel to remove most of the skins. Grease sheet and return nuts close together in single layer on sheet.

In small heavy saucepan, combine sugar and water; cook over medium heat until sugar dissolves. Increase heat to medium-high; boil for 5 to 8 minutes, without stirring, or until rich caramel color. Immediately pour over hazelnuts; let cool completely. Break into pieces. Chop in food processor. (Praline can be stored in airtight container for up to 5 days.)

In small saucepan, bring cream to boil; remove from heat and whisk in chocolate until melted completely. Whisk in liqueur until smooth. Stir in praline. Spread in plastic-wrap-lined 8-inch (2 L) square cake pan. Cover and refrigerate for at least 3 hours or overnight.

Holding plastic wrap, carefully remove from pan and place on cutting board; peel off wrap. With long sharp knife, cut into squares about 3/4-inch (2 cm). Sift cocoa lightly over top. Refrigerate in airtight container for up to 2 weeks or freeze for longer storage. Makes about 100 truffle squares.

When Sharon Boyd helps me test recipes, she brings not only wonderful laughter into my kitchen, but good ideas, too. It was hers to combine crunchy praline with a creamy, smooth truffle mixture in these decadent candies. They're true truffles, but putting the mixture in a pan and cutting it into tiny squares eliminates the tedious and messy task of rolling little balls.

THE WINE

The Pavlova is a tough match for any wine. I would suggest you end the meal the way you began it — with a bottle of champagne (but not Brut — Extra Sec or, if you can find it, Sec).

A cognac, Armagnac or an orange-based liqueur with Truffle Squares is a nice match.

INDEX